Übungsbuch

Compact Schülerhilfen

Englisch

Gebrauch der Zeiten

Beate Beck

Compact Verlag

Redaktion: Dorothee Wich, Birgit Schwarz, Sabine Walter
Umschlaggestaltung: Sabine Jantzen, Inga Koch
Illustration: Franz Gerg
Printed in Germany
ISBN 3-8174-7021-5
7370211

Inhalt

Wie du mit diesem Buch lernen kannst!

Grundvoraussetzung für gutes Englisch ist der richtige Gebrauch der Zeiten. Englische und deutsche Zeitformen unterscheiden sich wesentlich. Mit diesem Buch lernst du, diese Schwierigkeit zu meistern.

Im A-Teil findest du abwechslungsreiche Übungen zur richtigen Anwendung der verschiedenen Zeiten. Die wichtigsten Regeln und Besonderheiten werden hier wiederholt und intensiv eingeübt. Im B-Teil kannst du mit vermischten Tests deine Kenntnisse überprüfen und dich so gezielt auf Klassenarbeiten vorbereiten.

Die Übungsbücher bieten vielfältige und verständlich formulierte Aufgaben mit unterschiedlichem Schwierigkeitsgrad. Sie helfen dir, mögliche Fehler erfolgreich zu vermeiden und das Themengebiet sicher zu beherrschen.

Deinen Lernfortschritt kannst du sofort selbst kontrollieren: Bearbeite die Aufgaben Schritt für Schritt und vergleiche deine Ergebnisse mit den Lösungen am Ende des Buches!

Nun viel Erfolg!

Professor Magnus hilft dir, dich zurechtzufinden:

= Aufgabe: Alle Aufgaben solltest du schriftlich in einem gesonderten Arbeitsheft lösen.

= Testaufgabe zur Wiederholung des Gelernten

Alle Aufgabenstellungen sind rot markiert.

A. ÜBUNGEN

1. Gegenwart

1.1 Simple present

Übung 1: ***Simple present*** wird verwendet, wenn man ausdrücken will, dass etwas während eines unbegrenzten Zeitraums **regelmäßig, manchmal** oder **nie** geschieht (Beruf, Hobby, Wohnort, Vorlieben, etc.).
Bilde bejahte Aussagesätze (+), verneinte Aussagesätze (–) oder Fragen (?). Beachte die Umschreibung mit *to do* in verneinten Sätzen und Fragen!

Mike's friends:
1. Mary/watch/always/the cartoons on Channel 4 (+)
2. she/like/German lessons (–)
3. she/do/her homework/carefully (–)
4. she/play/the guitar/quite/well (+)
5. Bob/live/in the green house in Mansion Road (?)
6. he/be/a member of the hockey team (?)
7. he/play/hockey (+)
8. he/like/football (–)

Übung 2: ***Simple present*** wird auch verwendet, wenn man **aufeinander folgende Handlungen** aufzählt:
Zähle die ersten zehn Dinge auf, die du morgens nach dem Aufstehen machst:

At first I ..., then ...

Übung 3: **Present progressive** (present tense von *to be + -ing*) drückt aus, dass eine Handlung nur von **begrenzter Dauer** ist und sich **gerade (im Moment des Sprechens) im Verlauf** befindet. Signalwörter sind *at the moment, (right) now* (gerade jetzt), *just* (gerade), *look* (schau mal).
Setze folgende Verben im *present progressive* in der richtigen Reihenfolge ein, um die Sätze sinnvoll zu ergänzen: *smile, sit, rain, not do, carry, dream, look.*

At the moment Mary ... at her desk. But she ... her homework. She ... out of the window. Right now it ... . All the streets are wet and everybody ... an umbrella. ... Mary ... of her holidays in Spain? I think so. Look, she ... .

Übung 4: Unterstreiche erst die Signalwörter und setze dann die Verben in die richtige Form:

1. Mike and Mary ... (see) each other every day.
2. Pat often ... (write) letters to her German pen friend.
3. At the moment she ... (listen) to a CD with German songs.
4. She ... always ... (not understand) the texts.
5. Usually she ... (look up) the unknown words in her dictionary.
6. Right now ... (look for) a word she doesn't know.
7. Susan never ... (sleep) long on Sunday mornings.

Übung 5: Simple present oder *present progressive*? Streiche die falsche Form aus:

1. Peter lives / is living in London. But at the moment he works / is working in Birmingham.

2. Look, Julie bakes / is baking a cake. She invites / is inviting her friends once a month.
3. It often rains / is often raining in this part of the country.
4. Many students go / are going to school by bike every day.
5. Listen! The Back Street Boys sing / are singing their new song. I buy / I'm buying every new CD they publish.
6. Where's Mike? – He talks / is talking to Mary. He calls / is calling her every evening at this time.
7. What do you look / are you looking for? – I can't find my glasses. Usually they lie / are lying on my desk.

Übung 6: Nun bilde selbst die richtige Form:

1. Listen to this noise. It ... *(come)* from outside.
2. That's Dad. He ... *(mow = mähen)* the grass.
3. But he never ... *(mow)* the lawn *(Rasen)* on Fridays. He always ... *(do)* it on Saturday.
4. He ... *(test)* the new lawn-mower, you know. But obviously it ... *(not work)* correctly. It ... *(still/make)* too much noise.

Übung 7: Einige Verben können die ***progressive form*** normalerweise nicht bilden, weil sie etwas „Andauerndes" ausdrücken:
to like, to love, to hate, to feel (**Gefühle**)
to see, to hear, to smell (**sinnliche Wahrnehmung**) – aber: *I'm looking at* (anschauen), *I'm listening to* (an-, zuhören)
to believe, to know, to remember (sich erinnern), *to think, to understand* (**Denken und Meinen**)
to have, to contain, to possess, to belong (**Besitz**) – aber: *I'm having fun / a shower...* (Tätigkeit!)
to mean (bedeuten), *to need, to want, to be*
Setze die richtige Form ein:

1. Mary ... *(hate)* soap operas, but most of her friends ... *(watch)* them every evening on TV.

2. At the moment Mary ... *(want)* to talk to her friend Susan about the new boy at school, but Susan ... *(not listen)*. She only ... *(see)* what ... *(go on)* on the screen.
3. Peter ... *(like)* his girlfriend Susan very much. He ... *(call)* her as often as possible. At the moment he ... *(try)* to find a nice birthday present for her. Suddenly he ... *(hear)* that they ... *(play)* her favourite song on the radio. Now he ... *(know)* what to buy for her.
4. Hurry up. The taxi ... *(wait)*. – I ... *(know)*, but I ... *(look)* for my keys. ... *(you/remember)* where I put them?
5. John is in hospital for two weeks. Fortunately he ... *(have)* some good friends who ... *(visit)* him every day.
6. You ... *(not need)* a new sweatshirt, Mary. You already ... *(have)* enough. And we bought the one you ... *(wear)* only last week.

Übung 8: Auch Verben, die nur **ganz kurze Vorgänge** beschreiben *(to stop, to begin, to start, to open ...)*, stehen normalerweise **nicht** in der **progressive form**.
Entscheide, ob das Verb im *simple present* oder *present progressive* steht:

Mike ... *(switch on)* the TV. His favourite programme ... *(begin)*.
The criminal ... *(stop)* at a red traffic light. In front of him three cars ... *(wait)*. Suddenly he ... *(hear)* the police behind him. He ... *(fetch)* his gun and ... *(jump)* out of the car. A lot of people ... *(watch)* the scene but he ... *(disappear)* in the crowd.

Übung 9: Da wir im Deutschen die Unterscheidung zwischen *simple* und *progressive form* nicht kennen, musst du bei der Übersetzung ganz genau überlegen, welche Form du brauchst:

1. Ich kann nicht ans Telefon gehen *(to answer the phone)*. Ich dusche gerade.

2. Peter geht jeden Monat zwei oder drei Mal ins Kino.
3. Mike will sich ein neues Mountainbike kaufen. Deshalb spart *(to save)* er sein Taschengeld.
4. Als sich die Türen öffnen, warten vor der Konzerthalle schon Hunderte von Fans.
5. Ich bin nicht sicher, ob er schon schläft. Wahrscheinlich hört er seine CDs.
6. Erinnerst du dich an Jane? Sie sieht wie Madonna aus.
7. Wo wohnt *(to live)* dein Freund? – Er wohnt in London. Aber zur Zeit wohnt *(to stay)* er bei *(with)* seinem Onkel in Birmingham.
8. Normalerweise erzählt er immer *(always)* Witze. Aber heute fühlt er sich schlecht.
9. Meistens *(mostly)* scheint hier die Sonne. Wie schade *(what a pity)*, dass es heute regnet. Aber wir haben trotzdem *(nevertheless)* viel Spaß zusammen.
10. Hör nur! Der Hund bellt. Er hört, dass Bob nach Hause kommt. Bob geht jeden Abend mit ihm spazieren.

2. *Zukunft*

2.1 Will-future

Übung 10: **Will-future** wird verwendet,
- um auszudrücken, dass etwas stattfinden wird, ohne dass der Sprecher es beeinflussen kann,
- um Vermutungen wiederzugeben (häufig nach *I'm sure, I think, I believe, perhaps)* und nach *I hope*,
- wenn man sich spontan zu etwas entschließt.

Entscheide, ob das Verb im *simple present* oder *will-future* stehen muss:

1. ... *(you/know)* that Bob ... *(go)* to New York next week?
2. Peter's CD-player ... *(not work)* any more. He ... *(hope)* he ... *(get)* a new one for his birthday.
3. Pat ... *(attend)* German lessons at the youth club every Friday. So you ... *(not see)* her tonight.
4. He ... *(want)* to be alone. So nobody ... *(find)* him.
5. Oh Pat, we ... *(write)* a German test tomorrow. I ... *(be)* afraid that I ... *(be not able to)* answer the questions. – No problem, Mary. I ... *(explain)* the grammar to you, if you ... *(want)*.

Übung 11: Anders als im Englischen kann man im Deutschen auch das Präsens verwenden, wenn man über Ereignisse in der Zukunft spricht.

Übersetze die folgenden Sätze. Entscheide, ob du ***present tense oder will-future*** verwenden musst. Achte darauf, dass in temporalen Nebensätzen kein *will-future*, sondern *present tense* steht.

1. Er kennt ihn ziemlich gut.
2. Der Koffer *(suitcase)* ist zu schwer für dich. Warte, ich helfe dir.

3. Das Konzert dauert *(to last)* zwei Stunden. Das bedeutet, dass wir nicht vor 23 Uhr zurück sind.
4. Er ist sicherlich müde, wenn er ankommt.
5. Ich bin ziemlich sicher, dass Peter das Spiel verliert. Er spielt schlecht Tennis.
6. Ich ruf dich morgen früh an, in Ordnung?
7. Ich lese den Brief, sobald ich ihn bekomme.
8. Lass uns einkaufen gehen. Die Geschäfte schließen bald.

Übung 12: Die **Verlaufsform** des *will-future* (***future progressive:** will + be + -ing)* verwendet man bei Handlungen, die sich zu einem bestimmten Zeitpunkt gerade im Verlauf befinden werden oder von denen man erwartet, dass sie in der Zukunft geschehen.
Bilde erst die bejahten Aussagesätze und dann die Frage (?) oder Verneinung (–):

1. Peter/work/at 9 am (?)
2. band/play/until midnight (–)
3. sun/shine/tomorrow (?)
4. Julia/wait/when we arrive (?)
5. the children/sleep/when grandma calls (–)
6. Susan/laugh/when she hears this (–)

Übung 13: *Will-future*: Entscheide, wo die *progressive form* möglich ist. Denke auch daran, dass manche Verben die Verlaufsform nicht bilden können!

1. Mike: Next week this time *(nächste Woche um diese Zeit)* we ... *(lie)* in the sun.
   Mary: It ... *(be)* a great holiday. We ... *(have)* much fun.
   Mike: We ... *(not do)* anything but relaxing and we ... *(not come)* back before the end of July.
   Mary: O.k. Call me at seven. My parents ... *(watch)* the news on TV and nobody ... *(listen)* to us.

2. Peter: That was a terrible accident. People ... *(know)* about it soon. They ... *(read)* it in the newspapers and they ... *(talk)* about it for a long time.
Susan: I ... *(not look)* at the photos. Otherwise I ... *(dream)* of them.

Übung 14: **Future perfect** *(will + have + past participle)* wird verwendet, um auszudrücken, dass eine Handlung **zu einem bestimmten Zeitpunkt in der Zukunft beendet** sein wird. Setze die Verben in Klammern ins *future perfect*:

Die Ferien sind bald vorbei. Was wird Pat in vier Woche schon alles getan haben?

Four weeks today *(heute in vier Wochen)*
I ... *(develop)* my holiday photos,
school ... *(start)* again,
I ... *(lose)* most of my sun tan,
I ... *(catch a cold)* in the rainy weather here,
I ... *(not forget)* any of the fun I had with Tony,
I ... *(write)* several letters to him.
But: ... Tony ... *(forget)* me?

Übung 15: Unterscheide: *Until* wird verwendet, wenn etwas bis zu einem Zeitpunkt andauert, *by* wird verwendet, wenn etwas bis zu diesem Zeitpunkt geschehen sein wird.
Setze die richtige Form ein *(future perfect* oder *future progressive)* und entscheide, ob ***until* oder *by*** richtig ist!

1. My parents ... *(wait)* for us until/by the concert is over.
2. The teacher will arrive soon. I hope I ... *(finish)* my homework until/by then.
3. Next Friday I ... *(know)* my boyfriend for four months.
4. This time next week we ... *(celebrate)* our final exam party.
5. Until/By this time next week we ... *(pass)* all our tests.

6. ... you ... *(finish)* the letter until/by six? You know the post office closes then!
7. He ... *(not suffer)* long from this accident. He ... *(recover)* until/by today three weeks. In the tournament next month he ... *(play)* as well as before.

2.2 Simple present, present progressive, going-to-future

Übung 16: ***Present simple*** verwendet man für die Zukunft, wenn Ereignisse durch Fahrpläne, Veranstaltungsprogramme etc. festgelegt sind.
Bilde Frage und Antwort. Antworte in ganzen Sätzen!

1. theatre/begin? – 8 p.m.
2. day/be/tomorrow? – Tuesday
3. next English course/start? – September
4. your football training/end/this evening – 6.30 p.m.
5. holidays/start/this year? – August 1st
6. we/meet/guide? – in front of the hotel

Übung 17: Wird das ***present progressive*** für die Zukunft verwendet, drückt es aus, dass etwas für einen bestimmten Zeitpunkt fest geplant oder vereinbart ist.
Bilde erst die Fragen und dann die Antworten:

Peter fragt Mike nach seinen Urlaubsplänen:

1. how long/stay
2. when/leave
3. go/alone
4. go/by train
5. stay/a youth hostel
6. where/first
7. take/diving course

Mike antwortet (in ganzen Sätzen!):
1. two weeks
2. on Thursday
3. with Mary
4. yes
5. camping site
6. coast
7. no

Übung 18: Werden *simple present* oder *present progressive* für die Zukunft verwendet, muss dies immer deutlich aus dem Kontext hervorgehen, oder es muss eine Zeitangabe vorhanden sein.
Entscheide, ob *simple present* oder *present progressive* verwendet werden muss:

1. Mary and I ... *(go)* to the open air concert this evening. – Oh, great! What time ... it ... *(start)*?
2. Do you know that Pat ... *(work)* as an au pair in Germany next year?
3. ... you ... *(come)* to the typing course, too? It ... *(start)* next Monday.
4. My exams ... *(start)* at 8 o'clock tomorrow morning. So I ... *(not go out)* with you this evening.
5. I know that Bob and Mike ... *(play)* in the school hockey team next Sunday. Susan and I want to come, but what time ... game ... *(start)*?

Übung 19: Statt des *will-future* wird das *going-to-future* für Vorhaben verwendet, die man schon länger geplant hat.
Erzähle, was du nächstes Wochenende vorhast:

I'm going to ...

Übung 20: *Will-future* oder *going to*? Streiche die falsche Form aus:

1. Mike will buy / is going to buy a present for Mary. She will be / is going to be 15 tomorrow.
2. Susan will paint / is going to paint a picture for her. I'm sure it will be / is going to be very good.
3. Mary will have / is going to have a party on Thursday. I hope we'll have / are going to have much fun.
4. She hopes it won't rain / isn't going to rain because she'll celebrate / is going to celebrate in the garden.
5. Oh, I can't come, I'm afraid. We'll write / are going to write a test next Friday and I must do it well. That's why I'll study / I'm going to study maths on Thursday evening.
6. That's a pity, Bob. But wait, I'll ask / I'm going to ask her if she can't have the party on Friday.

Übung 21: Übersetze folgende Sätze. Entscheide, welche Form des *future* du verwenden musst:

1. Bob und Mike machen heute Nachmittag einen Fahrradausflug. Kommst du auch mit, Mary? – Ich fürchte, ich muss lernen. Ich werde an meinem Schreibtisch sitzen, während ihr Spaß habt.
2. Ich habe den Bus verpasst, Mama. Jetzt werde ich zu spät zur Schule kommen. Wenn ich ankomme, wird die Stunde schon begonnen haben und der Lehrer wird die Hausaufgaben kontrollieren. – Ok, ich fahre dich mit dem Auto hin.
3. Hast du das Plakat gesehen, Mike? Nächsten Monat kommt unsere Lieblingsband. – Ich weiß. Ich werde mir morgen eine Karte kaufen. – Gute Idee. Ich komme mit.
4. Wie kommen wir ins Stadion? – Mit dem Bus. Er fährt um 18.33 Uhr. Wir müssen pünktlich da sein. Sonst verpassen wir das Konzert.

3. Vergangenheit

3.1 Past tense

Übung 22: Wie lautet das *simple past* zu diesen Verben?

I am, she breaks, they cut, we lie *(liegen!),* they say, it begins, you buy, they drive, I leave, he pays, I speak
I eat, he gives, you know, she teaches, you throw, they find, we hear, he thinks, she writes

Übung 23: ***Simple past*** verwendet man für Handlungen und Ereignisse, die in der Vergangenheit stattgefunden haben und **abgeschlossen** sind.
Bilde bejahte Aussagesätze (+), verneinte Aussagesätze (–) oder Fragen (?) im *simple past.* Beachte die Umschreibung mit *to do* in verneinten Sätzen und Fragen!

1. you/watch/the film/on TV/yesterday evening (?)
2. I/see/the accident (+)
3. Pat/do/German/at school (–)
4. Mike/get up/early/this morning (+)
5. Peter/play/the tennis match/yesterday (?)
6. Yes/but/he/win (–)

Übung 24: Simple past wird auch für aufeinander folgende Handlungen verwendet.
Setze die folgenden Verben im *simple past* ein: *read (2), sit, come, start, look, be (2), think, open, take, go*

Every evening, when Pat ... home from work she immediately ... to the letter box. Excitedly *(aufgeregt)* she ... it and ...

into it. And today there ... a letter in it. She slowly ... the letter out of the box and anxiously ... the sender's name. Yes, it ... his name. She ... the letter three times. "Oh yes," she ... happily. "He hasn't forgotten me." Immediately *(sofort)* she ... down at her desk and ... to write him back.

Übung 25: Befindet sich ein Vorgang zu einem bestimmten Zeitpunkt in der Vergangenheit noch **im Verlauf**, steht das Verb im ***past progressive*** *(past tense* von *to be + -ing).*
Bilde vollständige Sätze:

What were the friends doing yesterday evening?

1. Mike/ride/his mountain bike
2. Pat/study/for her German course
3. Mike and Mary/plan/holidays
4. Bob/go for a walk/with his dog
5. Susan/write/a letter/to Peter
6. Peter/watch TV/with his uncle

Übung 26: Verwandle die Sätze 1–3 von Übung 25 in Fragen und verneine die Sätze 4–6!

Übung 27: Häufig beschreibt das *past progressive* eine Art Hintergrundhandlung zu einer neu eintretenden Handlung, die im *simple past* steht. Gleichzeitig ablaufende Handlungen stehen beide im *past progressive*.
Entscheide, welche Form richtig ist:

1. We ... *(sit)* in the garden when it ... *(start)* to rain. So we ... *(run)* into the house.
2. Mike and Mary ... *(talk)* on the phone, while Mary's parents ... *(watch)* TV.
3. ... John ... *(drive)* too fast, when the accident ... *(happen)*?

4. Susan ... *(wait)* at the station when Peter ... *(arrive)* from Birmingham. He ... *(bring)* some beautiful flowers for her as a present.
5. All the others ... *(dance)* at the party on Susan's birthday. Only Pat ... *(not want)* to dance. She ... *(only think)* of Tony and their discussion.
6. Bob ... *(see)* the burglar while he ... *(go)* for a walk with his dog.
7. While Pat ... *(work)* as an au pair in Germany she ... *(meet)* a lot of interesting people.
8. We ... *(just have)* breakfast when the postman ... *(bring)* your letter.

Übung 28: Da wir im Deutschen die Unterscheidung zwischen *simple* und *progressive form* nicht kennen, musst du bei der Übersetzung ganz genau überlegen, welche Verbform du brauchst.
Übersetze die folgende Geschichte:

Es war Freitagabend. Frau Miller bereitete das Abendessen vor, als sie den Lärm hörte. Sie wollte ihren Mann rufen, aber er reparierte das Auto in der Garage.
Frau Miller verließ die Küche und ging ins Wohnzimmer. Während sie aus dem Fenster schaute, sah sie einen Mann, der auf das Haus zu lief *(to run towards)*. Er trug etwas in seinen Armen. Dann klopfte *(to knock)* er an die Tür.
Während Frau Miller überlegte, was sie machen sollte *(what to do)*, rief der Mann: „Bitte öffnen Sie die Tür. Dieser Hund blutet stark *(heavily)*." Frau Miller öffnete die Tür und sagte: „Kommen Sie herein. Sie haben Glück, mein Mann ist Tierarzt *(vet)*."
Und während Frau Miller ihren Mann holte *(to get)*, legte der Mann den Hund auf den Tisch. Während Herr Miller den Hund untersuchte *(to examine)*, suchte seine Frau nach einer Telefonnummer auf der Hundemarke *(dog licence disc)*. Der Besitzer vermisste den Hund schon, als Frau Miller ihn anrief. Er war froh, als er hörte, dass Herr Miller seinen Hund retten konnte.

3.2 Present perfect

Übung 29: ***Present perfect simple*** *(have + past participle)* wird verwendet, wenn ein Ereignis in der Vergangenheit irgendwann einmal (oder auch gar nicht) stattgefunden hat. Das Ereignis hat jedoch noch spürbare **Auswirkungen auf die Gegenwart**.
Bilde bejahte Aussagesätze (+), Fragen (?) oder Verneinungen (–):

1. Bob/close/the window (+) That's why it's so warm here.
2. John/clean/his shoes (–) They are still dirty.
3. It/stop/raining (?) I want to go for a walk.
4. We/see/the film (–) We don't know if it's good or bad.
5. Mike/find/his keys (+) We can go now.
6. Susan/buy/some bread (?) We need some for breakfast.
7. Peter/call/Susan/yet *(not...yet = noch nicht)* (–) She's still waiting.
8. Mary/wash/the dishes (+) She can go out with Mike now.
9. Susan isnt't here. She/go/shopping (+)
10. Your hair looks so different. you/be/to the hairdresser's (?)

Übung 30: *Present perfect simple* wird auch verwendet, wenn etwas gerade eben *(just)* oder immer wieder bis heute stattgefunden hat.
Denk daran, dass im Deutschen die Vergangenheit mit *sein* und *haben* gebildet werden kann. *Present perfect* wird immer mit *have* gebildet.
Übersetze:

1. Hast du ihn schon getroffen?
2. Er hat schon immer diese teuren Zigarren geraucht.
3. Bist du jemals *(ever)* in Amerika gewesen?
4. Ich habe das Auto diesen Monat noch nicht gewaschen.
5. Sie sind niemals Freunde gewesen.

6. Ich habe die Lösung *(solution)* noch nicht gefunden.
7. Wir sind gerade nach Hause gekommen.
8. Hast du deine Hausaufgaben schon gemacht?
9. Sie sind immer mit dem Taxi zum Bahnhof gefahren.
10. Joe hat nie in London gewohnt.

Übung 31: *Present perfect simple* wird auch verwendet, wenn ein Zustand bis in die Gegenwart andauert.
Mit *for* beschreibt man den Zeitraum, den der Zustand/Vorgang schon andauert, mit *since* den Zeitpunkt, an dem der Zustand/Vorgang begonnen hat.
Setze das Verb ins *present perfect* und entscheide, ob *since* oder *for* richtig ist.

1. Peter ... *(be)* in Birmingham for/since three months now. He ... *(feel)* quite well for/since he went there.
2. Bob ... *(play)* all the matches for the hockey team for/since last summer.
3. But he ... *(not come)* to the training for/since three weeks.
4. Mike ... *(want)* to buy this mountain bike for/since months now.
5. Susan ... *(plan)* to go to Berlin for/since almost a year now.
6. She has ... *(already/read)* a lot of informative books about Germany.
7. Mike and Mary ... *(know)* each other for/since 1996.
8. She ... *(like)* him for/since they met for the first time.

Übung 32: Entscheide, ob *simple past* oder *present perfect simple* verwendet werden muss. Denk daran, dass das *simple past* eine genaue Zeit- oder Ortsangabe verlangt.

1. We didn't see / haven't seen you at Mary's party last Saturday, Mike. – Yes, we visited / have visited my grandparents.

2. Did you see / Have you seen Peter this week? – No, he is in Birmingham.
3. I didn't finish / haven't finished my homework yet. I can't go out now. – You're quite slow, Mary. I finished / have finished my homework an hour ago.
4. Do you know when Henry VIII became / has become King of England? I need to know this for my history lesson.
5. Did you ever go / Have you ever gone by plane? – Yes, last year, when we went / have gone to Spain.
6. They opened / have opened a new youth club. Let's go there tonight. – When did they open / have they opened it? – Last week.
7. Where did you buy / have you bought this great T-shirt, Susan? – Oh, it's nice, isn't it? I got / have got it at the fashion shop in Grant Street.
8. The band that played / has played at the school party is really great. I never heard / have never heard such an excellent amateur band.
9. I'm sorry, but Bob just left / has just left. Mike called / has called ten minutes ago. They want to play football.
10. Where did they go / have they gone? – No idea, I didn't ask / haven't asked them when they left / have left.

Übung 33: Jetzt setze selbst die richtigen Formen in folgendem Gespräch ein:

1. Mike: Last week I ... *(see)* a film about Germany. What about going on hoilday there?
2. Mary: That's a great idea. I ... *(want)* to go there since we ... *(start)* to learn German at school. But I ... *(never have)* enough money.
3. Mike: Well, I ... *(save)* some money since my last birthday. And we can stay at youth hostels. When our parents ... *(spend)* their holidays there years ago they ... *(be)* very simple places to sleep. But they ... *(become)* much more comfortable since then. Bob ... *(meet)* a lot of interesting people since he ... *(start)* to stay at youth hostels during his holidays.

4. Mary: And I'll ask mum. She ... *(promise)* to give me some money for the hoildays. And I ... *(get)* some good marks this school year. In the last German test I ... *(be)* the second-best.

Übung 34: **Present perfect progressive** *(have + been + -ing)* beschreibt den Verlauf einer Handlung, die in der Vergangenheit begonnen und noch nicht oder gerade erst zu Ende gegangen ist.
Bilde folgende Fragen und gib die Antworten mit *since* oder *for:*

1. how long/you/wait? – one minute
2. how long/the sun/shine? – this morning
3. how long/the baby/cry? – midnight
4. how long/Pat/learn/German? – a long time
5. how long/you/listen/to the radio? – I woke up this morning.
6. how long/Bob and Mike/jog? – one hour

Übung 35: Im Deutschen steht oft das Präsens! Übersetze die folgenden Sätze ins Englische und achte besonders auf den Gebrauch der Zeiten:

1. Pat schreibt schon seit einer Stunde an ihre deutsche Brieffreundin.
2. Bob spielt seit heute Nachmittag mit seinem Hund.
3. Wir warten seit einer halben Stunde auf den Bus zum Fußballstadion.
4. Mike und Mary planen seit Wochen ihre Ferien in Deutschland.
5. Peter sucht sein Portemonnaie, seit er von der Schule zurückgekommen ist.
6. Seit Abfahrt des Zuges steht Jenny.
7. Du isst seit Stunden Schokolade.
8. Ich freue mich seit Tagen auf deinen Besuch.

Übung 36: Entscheide, ob du *present perfect simple* oder *present perfect progressive* brauchst.
Bedenke, dass manche Verben die Verlaufsform nicht bilden!

1. Mike and Mary ... *(hitch-hike)* ... *(seit Stunden)*. But they ... *(not get)* a lift yet.
2. We ... *(not wait)* for the taxi for a long time. It ... *(just/ arrive)*.
3. Mike and Bob ... *(play)* hockey ... *(seit dem Frühstück)*. Now they are wet through.
4. Where is Susan? I ... *(look)* for her ... *(seit einer halben Stunde)*. – I don't know. I ... *(not see)* her today.
5. Our neighbour ... *(mow)* the grass ... *(seit)* I came home from school. He ... *(not finish)* yet.
6. ... *(Mike/do)* his homework yet? – No, he ... *(talk)* with Mary on the phone ... *(seit dem Mittagessen)*
7. Do you hear from Joe sometimes? – No, I ... *(not hear)* from him ... *(seit)* he left London last year.
8. Peter ... *(lie)* in bed ... *(seit Sonntag)*. But his influenza ... *(not get)* better yet.

Übung 37: Bei der Übersetzung ist es schwierig zu erkennen, ob man *past tense* oder *present perfect*, *simple form* oder *progressive form* verwenden muss. Die Form des deutschen Verbs hilft nicht weiter! Schau dir also den Satz genau an: Ist eine Zeitangabe für eine abgeschlossene Handlung vorhanden, darf nie *present perfect* stehen! Übersetze:

1. Als Pat auf dem Land *(in the country)* lebte, ging sie abends nicht oft aus. Jetzt lebt sie seit einem Jahr in London, ist schon oft in die Disko gegangen und hat einen Deutschkurs besucht *(to attend)*.
2. Hast du schon den neuen Film gesehen? – Ja, ich habe ihn letzte Woche mit Mike gesehen.

3. Seit wann kann *(to be able!)* Pat so gut Deutsch sprechen? – Sie hat letzten Sommer als Au-pair-Mädchen in München gearbeitet.
4. Ich habe noch nie eine so tolle CD gehört. Peter hörte sie auch gerade, als ich mit ihm telefonierte. – Ich weiß. Er hat sie mir zum Geburtstag geschenkt.
5. Peter hat seit drei Wochen eine neue Freundin. – Das stimmt nicht. Als ich gestern im Kino war, saß er mit Susan hinter mir.
6. Seit zwei Wochen haben wir jetzt schlechtes Wetter. Letztes Jahr war der Sommer sehr schön. Die Sonne hat fast die ganze Zeit geschienen.
7. Warum wollte Mike letzten Freitag nicht zur Party kommen? – Er streitet *(to quarrel)* seit drei Wochen mit Mary.
8. Ich habe gerade einen Kuchen gebacken. Möchtest du ein Stück? – Danke, ich habe seit Stunden nichts gegessen.
9. Seit wann *(Since when)* ist er an unserer Schule? – Ich weiß nicht. Ich habe ihn auch gerade zum ersten Mal gesehen. Aber er schaut uns schon die ganze Zeit an.

3.3 Past perfect

Übung 38: **Past perfect** wird verwendet, wenn eine Handlung bereits abgeschlossen war, als eine andere begann.
Lies die deutschen Sätze und unterstreiche die Satzteile, die im Englischen im *past perfect* stehen müssten.

1. Als er den Brief gelesen hatte, ging er ans Telefon.
2. Wir sprachen mit ihm, nachdem er nach Hause gekommen war.
3. Sie lachte, obwohl sie sich das Bein gebrochen hatte.
4. Wir konnten ihm erst helfen, als er uns alles erzählt hatte.
5. Nachdem wir eine Stunde lang gesucht hatten, fanden wir das Haus.
6. Sie kaufte sich ein Auto, weil sie viel Geld gewonnen hatte.
7. Er berichtete, was sich auf der Party ereignet hatte.

Übung 39: Beantworte folgende Fragen mit Hilfe der Angaben in Klammern. Verwende im Antwortsatz *simple past* und ***past perfect simple*** *(had + past participle):*

1. When did Peter call Susan?
   (after/he/arrive/Birmingham)
2. Why was Mike late for school?
   (because/miss/the bus)
3. Why didn't Mary go on the biking tour with her friends?
   (break/leg)
4. When did you buy this CD? (after/be/concert)
5. When did you fall in love with Mike?
   (after/we/dance/party)
6. Why didn't you write me a postcard?
   (because/forgotten/ your address)
7. Why didn't he go by car? (because/lost/his keys)
8. When did Pat go to Germany? (after/find/nice family)

Übung 40: Verbinde folgende Sätze mit Hilfe der Konjunktionen in Klammern. Eines der Verben muss jeweils im *past perfect simple* stehen.

1. Susan went to Birmingham. Peter invited her.
   (because)
2. Mike bought a new saddle for his bike. His father gave him the money. *(after)*
3. It was sunny for two weeks. It started to rain.
   (after)
4. Mike finally got the CD. He was in three shops.
   (after)
5. Pat was happy. Tony sent her a photo of himself.
   (because)
6. The burglar ran away. The alarm started to ring. *(because)*
7. Bob's dog Ronny came. Bob called him three times. *(after)*
8. They visited Mary in hospital. She broke her leg.
   (because)

Übung 41: Simple past oder *past perfect simple*?

1. Mary ... *(call)* Tony after she ... *(fetch)* the holiday photos.
2. Pat ... *(have)* no problems to find a good job after she ... *(be)* to Germany for one year.
3. She ... *(not forget)* her German friends after she ... *(return)* to England.
4. Susan ... *(like)* Peter before she ... *(meet)* him again at the party.
5. The woman ... *(called)* the police because she ... *(hear)* a strange noise in her neighbour's flat.
6. Later the police ... *(find out)* that it ... *(only be)* the cat.
7. The new boy ... *(not come)* to the party although Mary ... *(invite)* him.
8. Later he said: „I ... *(want)* to come, but I ... *(lose)* your address.“

Übung 42: **Past perfect progressive** *(had been + -ing)* wird verwendet, wenn ein Vorgang oder Zustand in der Vergangenheit beginnt und bis zu einem Zeitpunkt in der Vergangenheit andauert.
Entscheide, ob du das *past perfect simple, past perfect progressive* oder *simple past* brauchst:

1. They ... *(watch)* TV for two hours when their mother ... *(switch)* off the TV.
2. Mike ... *(learn)* English for three hours when his father ... *(say)* it was enough.
3. After I ... *(open)* the door, Peter ... *(come)* in quickly.
4. He was wet, because he ... *(walk)* through the rain for half an hour.
5. Before we ... *(visit)* Paris we ... *(read)* a lot of books about it.
6. The sun ... *(shine)* for weeks, but on the first day of our holidays it ... *(start)* to rain.
7. How long ... *(you/look)* for this sofa before you ... *(find)* it?

8. Pat and Tony ... *(know)* each other only for a few minutes. But they ... *(like)* each other at once.
9. She was completely out of breath. She ... *(run)* all the way after she ... *(hear)* the footsteps behind her.
10. They ... *(almost/give up)* hope when Peter finally ... *(arrive)*.

Übung 43: Entscheide zwischen *past tense* und *past perfect, simple* und *progressive*:

1. Bob ... *(just/come back)* from a walk with his dog, when Mike ... *(call)*. He ... *(try)* to reach Bob for more than an hour.
2. When Mike ... *(come)*, Mary and Susan ... *(already/look)* at the holiday photos for some time. Of course, Mike ... *(want)* to see them, too.
3. Susan ... *(paint)* her room since breakfast. So she ... *(be)* glad, when she ... *(get into bed)* in the evening.
4. When Mary ... *(come)* home from school all her friends ... *(wait)* for her. Mike ... *(organize)* a surprise birthday party for Mary.
5. Mike and Bob ... *(already/play)* hockey for half an hour, when their trainer ... *(arrive)*. He ... *(have)* an accident.
6. Mary ... *(do)* her homework when she ... *(remember)* that she ... *(promise)* Susan to go to the youth club that afternoon. They ... *(talk)* about this for days.

Übung 44: Denke daran, dass es im Deutschen die Verlaufsform nicht gibt, und dass man die Vorvergangenheit im Deutschen mit *sein* oder *haben* bilden kann, im Englischen aber nur mit *have*.
Übersetze:

1. Wir waren drei Stunden gelaufen, als es zu regnen begann.

2. Wir kannten Joe ziemlich gut, weil wir oft mit ihm gespielt hatten.
3. Nachdem der Trainer Peter eine Weile beobachtet hatte, durfte er in der Mannschaft spielen.
4. Pat erzählte die ganze Zeit von dem Jungen, den sie im Urlaub kennen gelernt hatte *(to meet)*.
5. Am Ende des Schulausflugs suchte Bobs Lehrer einige Jungen. Aber sie waren schon in den Bus gestiegen *(to get on)*.
6. Die Kinder waren müde. Sie waren den ganzen Tag draußen *(outdoors)* gewesen.
7. Sie konnte nicht glauben, dass es ihr gelungen war *(to succeed in doing s.th.)*, die Prüfung zu bestehen.

4. *Modale Hilfsverben*

4.1 Fähigkeit/Möglichkeit

Übung 45: Um eine **Fähigkeit** auszudrücken, verwendet man im *present tense* das Verb *can, cannot, can't,* im *past tense could, couldn't* oder *was / were able to* und in den anderen Zeiten (und als Infinitiv!) immer die Ersatzform *to be able to.*
Verwende die Ersatzform, um die folgenden Sätze in die angegebenen Zeiten zu setzen:

1. I can help you. (future)
2. We can't help them. (present perfect)
3. Mary can play volleyball again. (past tense)
4. The Walters can't find a new house. (past tense)
5. I can't come to your party. (present perfect)
6. Can they come? (future)
7. Pat doesn't sleep well. (present perfect)
8. Can she do her homework? (past tense)
9. We can't open the shop in time. (future)
10. The driver can stop in front of the child. (past perfect)

Übung 46: Im *past tense* verwendet man *was / were able to*, wenn man etwas in einer bestimmten Situation tun konnte. *Could* drückt eher eine allgemeine Fähigkeit aus. In verneinten Sätzen macht man diese Unterscheidung nicht, man kann also immer *couldn't* verwenden.
Entscheide, welche Form richtig ist!

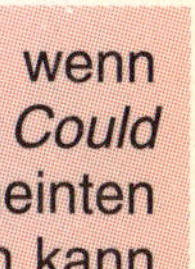

1. Pat could / was able to speak German, so she could / was able to ask her way when she was in Munich.
2. We could / were able to find a taxi, so we didn't have to walk.
3. When he was young, my father could / was able to run long distances.

4. I'm glad that I could / was able to get these tickets last week. I love this pop group.
5. The policeman ran after the thief and finally he could / was able to catch him.
6. Luckily our neighbour could / was able to describe the man who had broken into our house.
7. What a pity that Joe has moved away. He could / was able to tell such funny stories.
8. Yes, he could / was able to make people laugh. And he was the only one who could / was able to make Mary smile after her accident.

Übung 47: Mit *can* kann man auch eine **Möglichkeit** ausdrücken. *Could* kann dann *konnte (past tense)* oder *könnte (present tense)* bedeuten.
Übersetze den Ausdruck in Klammern:

1. ... you the CD. *(Ich kann nicht bringen)*
   ... it at my place, Mary? *(Könntest du abholen)*
2. ... Susan home, Mike? She doesn't feel well. *(Könntest du bringen)*
   ... alone. *(Sie kann nicht gehen)*
3. When we were young ... *(konnten wir nur wählen)* among two or three kinds of fruit.
4. ... to school by bus, but usually he walks. *(Peter könnte fahren)*
5. ... to him although he didn't have much time. *(Wir konnten sprechen)*
6. ... to me why you are late again? *(Kannst du erklären)*
7. ... a lot of interesting things in our holidays. *(Wir konnten sehen)*
8. ... you the photos we took, if you want. *(Wir können zeigen)*
9. ... earlier to the party because I went by bike. *(Ich konnte kommen)*
10. I would like to talk to her. ... me later? *(Könnte sie anrufen)*

Übung 48: Jetzt musst du auch überlegen, ob du die Ersatzform verwenden musst. Achte darauf, in welcher Zeit das Verb stehen muss und überlege besonders im *past tense*, ob es sich um eine allgemeine oder konkrete Fähigkeit oder um eine Möglichkeit handelt.
Übersetze:

1. Nachdem Pat den Deutschkurs besucht hatte, konnte sie ihre deutsche Brieffreundin viel besser verstehen.
2. Bis jetzt *(so far)* konnten wir nicht ins Ausland *(abroad)* fahren.
3. Aber nächstes Jahr werden wir uns einen Urlaub in Frankreich leisten können. *(s. etw. leisten = to afford s.th.)*
4. Letztes Jahr konnten wir auf einer Busreise *(coach tour)* ein paar interessante französische Städte besuchen. Ich könnte euch ein paar Informationen geben.
5. Aber wir konnten nicht alle Sehenswürdigkeiten besuchen. Die Zeit war zu knapp.
6. Mary konnte die Mathematikprüfung letzte Woche bestehen. Die Schüler konnten zwischen verschiedenen Aufgaben wählen.
7. Ich konnte ihn bis jetzt nicht erreichen. Könntest du mir seine neue Telefonnummer geben?
8. Pat wird Tony bald wieder sehen können. Er konnte seinen Chef überreden *(to persuade)*, ihn nach London fahren zu lassen.
9. Wir konnten bis jetzt keine Lösung finden. Ich hoffe, wir können Ihnen bald eine positive Antwort geben.

Übung 49: Auch *may* und *might* drücken eine Möglichkeit aus. In der Gegenwart bedeutet *might* eine geringere Wahrscheinlichkeit. Im Deutschen steht meistens *vielleicht.*
Übersetze:

1. Er hat vielleicht Recht *(to be right).*
2. Bob hat vielleicht den Bus verpasst.

3. Wir sehen ihn vielleicht nächsten Monat.
4. Er hat ihn vielleicht getroffen.
5. Joe wird vielleich bald schreiben.
6. Mary wollte vielleicht auch kommen.
7. Sie werden vielleicht nicht heiraten.
8. Wir finden vielleicht eine Lösung.

4.2 Erlaubnis/Verbot

Übung 50: Um eine Erlaubnis zu geben verwendet man ***can***, um ein Verbot auszusprechen ***mustn't***. Die Ersatzform für beide Hilfsverben ist ***(not) to be allowed to***.
Setze die folgenden Sätze in die angegebenen Zeiten:

1. Peter can go swimming with his friends.
   (future tense)
   (present perfect)
   (past tense)
2. Mary mustn't do so much sport after her accident.
   (future tense)
   (past tense)
   since her accident (present perfect)

Übung 51: May verwendet man nur, um höflich um Erlaubnis zu bitten *(May I...)* und in der Antwort darauf *(Yes, you may. No, you may not.)* Übersetze:

1. Darf ich Sie zum Abendessen einladen? – Ja.
2. Darf Susan heute Abend kommen? – Nein.
3. Dürfen wir Ihnen die Stadt zeigen? – Natürlich.
4. Darf ich dein Auto benutzen? – Nein.
5. Dürfen wir heute Abend später kommen? – Nein.
6. Darf ich mir dieses Buch kaufen? – Ja.

Übung 52: Entscheide, ob *may* in den folgenden Sätzen *dürfen* oder *vielleicht* bedeutet.

1. This may be Bob.
2. You may open your present now.
3. No, you may not watch that film on TV now.
4. Mary may not know this song.
5. We may go on a bike tour next Sunday.
6. Susan may watch TV until 10, but Robby must go to bed at 8 o'clock.
7. I have done my homework, so now I may play streetball with you.
8. We may meet them on the street.

Übung 53: *(Not) to be allowed to* wird auch im *present tense* verwendet, wenn man ausdrücken will, dass etwas ganz allgemein erlaubt oder verboten ist. Der Urheber der Erlaubnis oder des Verbots ist eine dritte Person oder nicht bekannt. Welche Form ist richtig?

1. I know, a lot of children can / are allowed to watch TV in the evenings, but you mustn't / aren't allowed to do that.
2. We mustn't / aren't allowed to smoke here in the museum.
3. O.k., you can / are allowed to go to school by bike today. It's warm enough. But remember you mustn't / aren't allowed to park your bikes in the school yard! There's a special place for them.
4. You mustn't / aren't allowed to let your dog run free here in the park.
5. Bob can / is allowed to come for the weekend. But he mustn't / isn't allowed to bring his dog. You know we mustn't / aren't allowed to have dogs here.
6. Can we have / Are we allowed to have some ice, Mrs Mayson? – I don't know if Peter can / is allowed to eat ice again after he was ill.

Übung 54: Verwende *can, may, may not, mustn't* oder die Ersatzform:

1. ... *(darf ich)* offer you a cup of tea?
2. Mary hopes she ... *(darf)* spend her holidays in Germany with Mike next summer.
3. Hurry up! You ... *(dürft nicht)* miss the hockey training again.
4. Peter and Mike ... *(dürfen)* come this afternoon, but you must look after your little brother, too.
5. When I was eight I ... *(durfte nicht)* to go out with friends in the evening.
6. ... *(dürfen wir)* go to school by bike? – No, you ... *(dürft nicht)*. You know that the streets are too dangerous.
7. Peter ... *(darf)* to drive a car since he got his driving licence two weeks ago.

Übung 55: Übersetze:

1. Susan durfte nicht zu Peters Party kommen, weil sie krank war.
2. Darf ich mir ein Stück Kuchen nehmen? – Natürlich. Bedien dich.
3. Wir können über alles reden, aber du darfst mich nicht anlügen *(lie to s.b.)*.
4. Man darf die Zeitschriften nicht lesen, wenn man sie nicht kaufen will.
5. Frau Johnson ist seit drei Tagen im Krankenhaus und wir durften sie noch nicht besuchen.
6. Glaubst du, dass du mit Mike in den Urlaub fahren darfst? – Ich hoffe, dass ich meine Eltern überzeugen kann.
7. In Großbritannien dürfen die Schüler in der Schule nicht die Kleider tragen, die sie wollen.
8. Darf ich mich hier hinsetzen? – Leider nicht. Der Platz ist besetzt.
9. Nein, du darfst nicht mit deinem Bruder ins Kino gehen. Kinder unter 16 dürfen diesen Film nicht anschauen.

4.3 Zwang/Notwendigkeit

Übung 56: Um zu sagen, dass jemand etwas tun muss, verwendet man *must*, wenn etwas nicht getan werden muss *needn't* (du brauchst nicht). Die Ersatzform ist *(not) to have to.* Was gibt den richtigen Sinn?

1. <u>You must/needn't wash the dishes</u>. Jack has already done it.
2. <u>You must/needn't be back on time</u> or you won't go out in the evening again.
3. I hope <u>we must/needn't use the first aid box</u> on our tour tomorrow, but you never know.
4. <u>You must/needn't help me</u> the whole afternoon, but <u>you must/needn't</u> at least clean up your room.
5. <u>Mike must/needn't look at his mother</u> to know that she's angry about his bad mark.
6. <u>Susan must/needn't do her homework</u> before she can play with you. So please come back later.

Übung 57: Nun setze die unterstrichenen Satzteile aus Übung 56 in die folgenden Zeiten:

1. future tense
2. past tense
3. present perfect
4. past tense
5. past tense
6. future tense

Übung 58: Übersetze die Ausdrücke in Klammern. Denke auch an die Ersatzform! Achtung: Im Deutschen sagt man auch *du musst* nicht statt *du brauchst nicht!*

1. We ... *(brauchten nicht)* pay to see the film at school. The entrance was free.

2. ... *(müssen wir)* show our passport at the airport?
3. Everybody ... *(musste)* bring something to drink to Mike's party.
4. You ... *(brauchst nicht)* complain about your bad marks at all. Study harder!
5. Since Mary broke her leg we ... *(müssen)* take her to school by car.
6. ... *(Musstet ihr)* go to the police after the accident? – Yes, of course. But we ... *(mussten nicht)* wait long.
7. You ... *(brauchst nicht)* look for your dog any more, Bob. He's in our garden. But you ... *(musst)* keep him on the lead next time.
8. He ... *(muss)* take these tablets for three weeks now.

Übung 59: Sehr häufig werden *mustn't* (nicht dürfen) und *needn't* (nicht müssen / nicht brauchen) verwechselt! Unterstreiche die richtige Form:

1. You mustn't/needn't be so noisy. The baby is sleeping.
2. You mustn't/needn't ask him for the way. He's a stranger.
3. We mustn't/needn't hurry. They will be waiting for us.
4. I really like pop concerts, but the music mustn't/needn't be too loud.
5. I haven't told anybody about it yet. And you mustn't/needn't tell anybody, either.
6. I'm not ready yet, but you mustn't/needn't wait for me. I'll come later.

Übung 60: *To have to* wird auch im *present tense* verwendet, wenn man ausdrücken will, dass nicht der Sprecher selbst, sondern äußere Umstände oder andere Personen etwas verlangen. Streiche die falsche Form aus:

1. It's so cold that we must / have to switch on the heating even though it is June.

2. Bob must / has to come home at once. I need him here to help me in the garden.
3. We must / have to visit him when he's back. He'll have a lot of nice photos.
4. We must / have to park the car a bit away from his house. Parking is not allowed in front of it.
5. You must / have to ask the caretaker if he has found your purse.
6. He must / has to look into all the classrooms at the end of a schoolday.

Übung 61: Übersetze:

1. Du brauchst die Heizung nicht anschalten *(to switch on)*. Es ist warm genug hier.
2. Letzte Woche musste Bob mit dem Hund zum Tierarzt gehen.
3. Das Konzert endet um Mitternacht. Wir müssen die Kinder mit dem Auto abholen.
4. Mein Vater wartet. Ich muss jetzt gehen. – Schade, aber du musst (noch) ein Stück Kuchen probieren. Du darfst nicht ohne gehen.
5. Meine Eltern sind sehr streng. Ich werde am Sonntag zu Hause bleiben müssen.
6. Der Service in dem Restaurant war sehr gut. Wir mussten nicht lange auf das Essen warten.
7. Du brauchst die Karten nicht kaufen, Peter. Ich werde sie holen können.
8. Mussten wir Mathe-Hausaufgaben machen? – Natürlich. Aber du brauchst sie jetzt nicht mehr abschreiben, der Lehrer kommt gerade.
9. Das Haus ist ziemlich alt. Wir werden alles renovieren müssen. – Du brauchst dir deswegen keine Sorgen machen. Unsere Freunde werden uns helfen.
10. Ich brauche heute nicht so früh aufstehen, weil Samstag ist.
11. Ihr müsst die Katze wegen der Leute mit Katzenallergie draußen lassen.

4.4 Sollen

Übung 62: Für *sollen* gibt es im Englischen mehrere Entsprechungen:
***Shall** I...?* (Soll ich...?): nur in der Frage nach einer Anweisung
*You **should / ought to*** (Du solltest ...): Ratschlag
*You **are to** come* (Du sollst ...): Anweisung einer dritten Person (Aber: Geht die Aufforderung vom Sprecher aus, heißt es you *must/mustn't* ...)
*He **is said to** be rich.* (Er soll reich sein / ist angeblich reich.)
Finde in folgenden Sätzen die richtige Entsprechung für *sollen*:

1. You ... *(sollt)* be at school on time. .... *(soll)* I take you there by car?
2. Peter ... *(soll)* be quite good at hockey. Is that true?
3. We ... *(sollten)* be careful with this dog. It looks dangerous.
4. Which way ... *(sollen)* we take? The left or the right one?
5. You ... *(solltest)* take an umbrella with you, Susan. It's going to rain.
6. We must see that film. It ... *(soll)* be great.
7. We ... *(sollten* Vergangenheit!*)* bring the English book. – Oh, I've forgotten it!
8. ... *(soll)* I help you with your homework? – No, thank you, we ... *(sollen)* do it on our own.
9. You ... *(sollt nicht)* run around on the coach while we are driving. It's too dangerous.
10. We .... *(sollten nicht)* wait any longer. He won't come any more.

Übung 63: Übersetze:

1. Du solltest nicht so lang fernsehen, Peter.
2. Wohin sollen wir das Klavier stellen?

3. Wo ist Mike? Er sollte vor einer halben Stunde hier sein. Wir sollten ihn anrufen.
4. Bobs Hund hat ihn angeblich gebissen. Stimmt das? – Unsinn. Du solltest Ronny sehen. Er ist ein braver *(good)* Hund.
5. Welche Bluse soll ich nehmen? – Keine Ahnung. Aber beeil dich. Wir sollen um drei zu Hause sein.
6. Du solltest nicht so lange mit deiner Antwort warten. Er wird angeblich sehr schnell ungeduldig *(impatient)*.
7. Ihr sollt jetzt mit den Hausaufgaben anfangen. Ihr sollt die Vokabeln morgen können.
8. Weißt du, was aus Joe geworden ist? – Er wohnt jetzt angeblich in New York.
9. Ihr solltet immer euren Lehrer fragen, ob ihr die Sätze auch aufschreiben sollt.

Übung 64: Das Passiv wird mit einer Form von ***to be*** und dem Partizip Perfekt *(**past participle**)* gebildet. Dabei wird das Hifsverb *to be* in die entsprechende Zeitstufe gesetzt:
Bilde Sätze im Passiv in den angegebenen Zeiten:

1. photo/make/last year – past tense
2. song/play/quite often/on the radio – present tense
3. new information/just/give – present perfect
4. a lot of people/invite/to the party – past perfect
5. their new CD/publish *(veröffentlichen)*/next month – will-future
6. car/can/repair – present tense
7. ambulance/call – present perfect
8. problem/solve/soon – will future

Übung 65: Nun verneine (–) die Sätze der Übung 64 oder bilde Fragen (?):

1. When ... (?)
2. ... (–)
3. ... (?)
4. ... (?)
5. ... (–)
6. ... (–)
7. ... (?)
8. ... (?)

Übung 66: Die **Verlaufsform** des Passivs gibt es nur im *present tense* und im *past tense.* Sie wird mit der entsprechenden Form von *to be + being + past participle* gebildet.
Setze folgende Sätze in die Verlaufsform:

1. The exhibition is opened.
2. The little dog was punished.
3. Are the windows cleaned?

4. Was the wall painted?
5. Is the dog taken for a walk?
6. The injured man is helped.
7. The stew ist cooked.
8. The film was shown in the assembly hall.

Übung 67: Ist der Verursacher der Handlung (eine Person oder eine Sache) bekannt und wichtig (also nicht *somebody, they, ...*), wird er mit *by* an das Verb angeschlossen ***(by-agent)***. Lies folgende Sätze durch und kreuze die an, in denen der Handlungsverursacher wirklich bekannt bzw. wichtig ist.

1. They don't sell tickets before the concert.
2. Did Mary invite the new boy to the party?
3. Will they renovate the school building?
4. They haven't found Ronny's dog yet.
5. Thousands of people had visited the exhibition before it closed.
6. A little boy called the ambulance.
7. They have planned the surprise party very carefully.
8. A big lorry caused the accident.
9. Can they repair your car?
10. They were just closing the shop when I arrived.
11. A letter informed him about his winnings in the lottery.
12. Did Peter organize the concert?

Übung 68: Nun wandle die Sätze aus Übung 67 ins Passiv um. Dabei wird das **Objekt des Aktivsatzes** zum **Subjekt des Passivsatzes**. Vergiss das *by-agent* nicht!

Übung 69: Ins Deutsche wird das *by* mit *von* oder *durch* übersetzt. Übersetze die Sätze 2, 5, 6, 8, 11 und 12 der Übung 68 ins Deutsche.

Übung 70: Wenn du deutsche Sätze mit einer Form von *werden* ins Englische übersetzt, musst du folgende Bedeutungen unterscheiden:
Er wird kommen. (Aktiv, *will-future*)
Er wird (gerade) gerufen. (Passiv, *present tense simple/progressive)*
Er wird bald gerufen (werden). (Passiv, *will-future*).
Übersetze die folgenden Sätze:

1. Wird die Schule bald renoviert werden?
2. Diese Frage wird von den Eltern oft gestellt. *(to ask a question)*
3. Wir werden in den nächsten Ferien anfangen.
4. Die Schüler werden helfen.
5. Die Klassenzimmer werden von den Schülern gestrichen.
6. Die Eltern werden durch einen Brief genau informiert werden.
7. Geldspenden *(donations)* werden schon in diesem Monat benötigt.
8. Ein Konto *(bank account)* wird gerade eröffnet.
9. Die Renovierung wird auch durch die Zeitung unterstützt *(support)* werden.
10. Das neue Dach wird vom Stadtrat *(town council)* bezahlt.

Übung 71: Ist das Verb eng mit einer Präposition verbunden, muss diese im Passivsatz **direkt beim Verb** stehen.
Bilde Sätze im Passiv. Manchmal brauchst du das *by-agent!*
Bilde vollständige Sätze:

1. Bob/wake up/dog/last night
2. the burglar/chase away *(verjagen)*/dog – past perfect
3. new locks/put in/tomorrow
4. It's cold outside. heating *(Heizung)*/must/turn on
5. injured boy/look after/nurse – present progressive!
6. he/must/operate on the arm?

Übung 72: Forme die folgenden Sätze vom Aktiv ins Passiv um:

1. Peter's boss has sent him to Birmingham.
2. Susan hopes that Peter will ring her up soon.
3. They have already filled in the forms.
4. Everybody must take off their shoes.
5. They have cut down these beautiful old trees.
6. You know that you must pay back the money.
7. You mustn't throw away these papers.
8. The police shot down the thief.
9. A drunken driver ran over the cat.
10. They will report on the accident in the local newspaper.

Übung 73: Bei Verben mit zwei Objekten kann sowohl das direkte Objekt (meist eine Sache) als auch das indirekte Objekt (meist eine Person) des Aktivsatzes Subjekt des Passivsatzes werden. In den meisten Fällen wird die Person zum Subjekt des Passivsatzes (= persönliches Passiv).
Setze die folgenden Aktivsätze ins Passiv. Beginne die Sätze, wie es vorgegeben ist. Manchmal musst du das *by-agent* verwenden:

1. Mary is just showing us some holiday photos.
   We ...
2. The company pays Peter more money because he has gone to Birmingham.
   Peter ...
3. They'll sent Pat the au pair family's address next week.
   Pat ...
   The au pair family's address ...
4. They had already sent her a lot of useful information about her stay in Germany.
   She ...
   A lot of useful information ...

5. The members of the committee were asking her a lot of questions in the interview.
   She ...
6. Miks's parents gave him the rest of the money for his mountain bike.
   Mike ...
   The rest of the money ...
7. Joe himself has sent his friends these photos of New York.
   Joe's friends ...
   These photos of New York ...

Übung 74: Auch wenn das Passiv möglich wäre, verwendet man im Deutschen oft eher eine Konstruktion mit *man*, wenn der Handlungsverursacher nicht bekannt ist.
Übersetze folgende Sätze, verwende aber das Passiv:

1. Man bringt ihn gerade nach Hause.
2. Man hat Mary gestern am Bein operiert.
3. Man hat Mike zum Mannschaftskapitän *(team captain)* gewählt *(to elect)*.
4. Man wird alle Einwohner einladen.
5. Man befragt gerade alle Anwohner *(residents)*, ob sie den Einbrecher gesehen haben.
6. Man wird den Einbrecher finden.
7. Man wird das neue Einkaufszentrum morgen eröffnen.
8. Man hat alle alten Häuser renoviert.

Übung 75: Bei der Übersetzung ins Deutsche versucht man aus stilistischen Gründen, Passivkonstruktionen zu vermeiden. Verwende daher bei folgenden Sätzen aus Übung 73 eine aktive Konstruktion mit *man* bzw. dem Handlungsverursacher als Subjekt:

1. We are just being shown some holiday photos by Mary.
2. The new adress will be sent to Pat next week.

3. A lot of useful information had already been sent to her.
4. She was being asked a lot of questions by the members of the committee.
5. Mike was given the rest of the money by his parents.
6. These photos of New York have been sent to Joe's friends by Joe himself.

Übung 76: Übersetze die folgenden Sätze ins Englische. Verwende immer das Passiv:

1. Man hat Mike gestern ein gebrauchtes Mountainbike angeboten.
   Mike ...
   A used mountain bike ...
2. In der Touristeninformation zeigte man Pat den Weg zum Bahnhof auf dem Stadtplan.
   At the ... Pat ...
3. Diese Geschichte hat mir immer meine Großmutter vorgelesen.
   This story ...
4. Die Nachbarin hat Mike £3 versprochen, wenn er ihren Rasen mäht.
   Mike ...
5. Die geretteten Touristen dankten den Helfern.
   The helpers ...
6. Die Getränke sind schon von diesem Herrn bezahlt worden.
   The drinks ...
7. Der ganze Strand ist durch Öl verunreinigt worden.
8. Man sagt, dass Joe jetzt in New York lebt.
   Joe ..
9. Man hat ihr versprochen, dass sie in zwei Wochen wieder zu Hause ist.
10. Man wird ihnen zeigen, wie sie sich schützen können.
11. Nach der Eröffnung dankte man dem Minister für seine Rede.
12. Als Mary aus dem Krankenhaus nach Hause kam, hat man ihr in der Schule sehr geholfen.

Übung 77: Bei der Bildung des Passivs kann man viele Fehler machen. Finde und verbessere sie in den folgenden Sätzen:

1. The new cinema is opened next week.
2. Mike has already be given a lot of presents for his birthday.
3. The exercise was explained to us from our teacher.
4. At the moment the dog is fed by Ronny.
5. The soup must being taken off the oven at once.
6. A lot of houses were damaged through the storm.
7. The heating has be turned on. Now it's warm enough.
8. The woman could been saved.
9. The doors are just been opened.

Übung 78: Steht das Verb, das die indirekte Rede einleitet, im ***present tense, present perfect*** oder ***future tense***, wird die Zeitstufe der direkten Rede in der indirekten Rede beibehalten. Die Personalpronomen, Possessivbegleiter u.s.w. müssen jedoch immer dem Standpunkt des Sprechers angepasst werden.
Setze folgende Aussagesätze in die indirekte Rede:

1. "I can't find my purse. I must have lost it somewhere."
   She has just told me that ...
2. "I can't come to your birthday party."
   Look, she is just telling her that ...
3. "My friend doesn't like dancing."
   She always complains *(sich beklagen)* that ...
4. "I saw Fred at the youth club with his new girlfriend."
   (Mike to Fred:) She tells everybody ...
5. "You haven't brought my CD back yet."
   That's not right. I'm sure that ...
6. "You'll miss a great concert if you don't come with us, Mary."
   Mary: I know that ...
7. "I don't want to see you again."
   O.k. I already know that ...

Übung 79: Setzt man eine **Frage** in die indirekte Rede, ändert sich die Satzstellung: Aus dem Fragesatz wird ein Aussagesatz. Das Fragewort wird jedoch beibehalten. Ist kein Fragewort vorhanden (Entscheidungsfragen), wird die indirekte Form mit *if* oder *whether* (ob) eingeleitet.
Setze folgende Fragen in die indirekte Rede:

1. "When are you leaving for Dresden, Pat?"
   I'd like to know ... you ...

2. "Where did she buy this sweatshirt?"
   I must ask her ...
3. "Has she known him long?"
   I wonder ...
4. "Are we to do the English homework for tomorrow?"
   I'm not sure ...
5. "Where does Peter work?"
   Do you know ...
6. "How much did you pay for the bike?"
   Why don't you tell me ...
7. "Why didn't you come to the hockey match?"
   He will ask me ...
8. "What's the time, please?"
   Can you tell me ...
9. "Will they find the way to our house?"
   They are surely wondering ... we ...
10. "When did you leave your house?"
    The police inspector has just asked me ...

Übung 80: Enthalten direkte Fragen mit *I* oder *we* ein **modales Hilfsverb**, können sie in der indirekten Form verkürzt durch **Fragewort + Infinitiv** wiedergegeben werden. Für *ob* kann in diesem Fall nur *whether* (nicht *if!)* verwendet werden. Welche der folgenden Fragen können in der indirekten Form verkürzt werden?

1. When shall I meet him this evening?
2. Why don't you ask him?
3. Have we got enough tea and bread?
4. Where could we find a suitable flat?
5. Have you finished the book yet?
6. How can we explain this to Peter?
7. Must we tell him the truth?
8. Why should we explain anything to him?
9. Did you see him last week?
10. When can you bring me the CD?
11. What will Mr Miller tell us?

Übung 81: Nun verkürze die Fragen aus Übung 80, bei denen dies möglich ist:

1. She doesn't know ...
4. We are not sure ...
6. We must decide ...
7. I'm not sure ...
8. I wonder ...

Übung 82: Im Deutschen ist diese Verkürzung nicht möglich. Übersetze und verwende – wenn möglich – die Kurzform:

1. Ich frage mich, wann ich diesen Brief schreiben soll.
2. Er möchte wissen, wann er am Bahnhof sein soll.
3. Sie weiß nicht, ob ihr Fahrrad repariert werden kann.
4. Kannst du mir sagen, wo meine Hose ist?
5. Ich weiß nicht, wie ich dir helfen kann.
6. Jeder fragt mich, wann die Party anfängt.
7. Ich weiß nicht, ob du diese Frage beantworten sollst.
8. Sag mir bitte, wann ich dich anrufen soll.
9. Ich bin nicht sicher, ob er auch kommen wird.
10. Ich frage mich, warum du da bist.

Übung 83: Nun übersetze die englischen Sätze ins Deutsche:

1. Let's ask him when to collect him at the airport.
2. She doesn't know whether to put on a coat.
3. John has asked me if I can lend him my new bike.
4. I would like to know how to put up this cupboard.
5. We will know very soon if he has passed the exam.
6. Please show me where to put my suitcases.
7. Do you know since when Ann has been back?
8. We have no idea where to spend our holidays this year.

Übung 84: Auch **Aufforderungen und Befehle** werden in der indirekten Rede durch eine **Infinitivkonstruktion** wiedergegeben. Einleitende Verben sind *to tell/order s.b. to do s.th., to ask s.b. to do s.th. (jdn. bitten etw. zu tun).* Ein Verbot erfolgt mit *to tell/order not to do s.th.*
Bilde die indirekte Rede:

1. “Give me the book.” – The teacher tells Mary ...
2. “Clean the glasses carefully.” – Mrs Elliot tells her son ...
3. “Don’t use my bike.” – Peter orders his little brother ...
4. “Open the window.” – Mr Mason asks a pupil ...
5. “Don’t come home late.” – Mr Brown orders his daughter ...
6. “Please give me some advice.” – Mary asks Susan ...
7. “Don’t forget to show your parents the letter.” Mr Mason tells his class ...
8. “Please tell us a story.” – Nellie asks her grandpa ...
9. “Bring some milk if you go to the supermarket.” – Mary’s mother orders her ...
10. “Don’t put on your new shoes.” – And she tells her ...

Übung 85: Nun übersetze die indirekten Befehle/Verbote aus Übung 84 ins Deutsche.

Übung 86: Übersetze ins Englische:

1. Peters Mutter sagt ihm, dass er das Radio lauter stellen soll.
2. Frau Simson bittet Mike ihre Tasche zu tragen.
3. Toms Vater hat ihm verboten *(to tell)*, mit dem Fahrrad zur Schule zu fahren.
4. Ich habe dir immer wieder gesagt, dass du die Schlüssel mitnehmen sollst.
5. Warum bittest du ihn nicht dich anzurufen?
6. Bitte sag ihm, dass er Blumen kaufen soll.

7. Bob befiehlt seinem Hund den Ball zurückzubringen.
8. Der Arzt rät *(to advise)* Mary, eine Woche im Bett zu bleiben.
9. Er sagt ihr, dass sie nicht herumlaufen soll.
10. Wir müssen Kate bitten uns ihr Zelt zu leihen.

Übung 87: Steht das Verb, das die indirekte Rede einleitet, in der **Vergangenheit**, musst du eine weitere wichtige Regel beachten: Die Zeitstufe des Verbs der indirekten Rede wird gegenüber dem Verb der direkten Rede um eine Zeitstufe in die Vergangenheit zurückversetzt *(backshift of tenses)*. Daraus ergibt sich folgende **Zeitverschiebung**: *present tense → past tense, present perfect → past perfect, past tense → past perfect, will → would, can → could, may → might; should* und *could* bleiben unverändert. Beachte das einleitende Verb und entscheide, welche Form des Verbs richtig ist:

1. "In Leeds we bought a new cupboard."
   Mrs Jackson told her neighbour that they bought / had bought a new cupboard in Leeds.
2. "Next month we'll fly to Paris."
   She also told her that they will fly / would fly to Paris next month.
3. "I can't help you."
   She has just told me that she can't/couldn't help me.
4. "The film isn't over yet."
   She shouted that the film isn't/wasn't over yet.
5. "I don't want to do my homework."
   Ben says that he doesn't/didn't want to do his homework.
6. "We haven't ordered anything."
   Mrs Brown told the postman that they haven't ordered / hadn't ordered anything.
7. "The school hockey team may be too bad."
   He had thought that the school hockey team may / might be too bad.

Übung 88: Nun setze selbst die richtige Form ein:

1. "Can you help me to prepare the party next Saturday?"
   Yesterday Peter asked Susan ... next Saturday.
2. "Peter will help you to find your purse."
   I'm sure ... to find your purse.
3. "I have been playing for the same football team for five years now."
   He told me ... for five years now.
4. "Has Ann already found a new flat?"
   I wanted to know ... a new flat.
5. "Yes, she lives in Manchester Road now."
   Her father told me ... in Manchester Road now.
6. "They are planning a new youth centre in our part of the town."
   Yesterday Mary told me excitedly ... a new youth centre in our part of the town.
7. "We could hide in a small hut when it started to rain."
   She explained to me ... in a small hut when ... to rain.
8. "I don't know the answer."
   The pupil must tell the teacher ... the answer.
9. "We were watching TV when we heard the strange noise."
   Mrs Jones told the police ... when ... the strange noise.
10. "Joe is going to New York very soon."
    Did you know ... very soon?

Übung 89: Setze das Verb in die richtige Zeit oder verwende den Infintiv!

1. "I may let you play in the next match, Mike."
   The team coach had told Mike ... in the next match.
2. "Don't walk alone in the streets at night."
   Mike mother told him ... in the streets at night.
3. "Where did you learn to speak German so well?"
   My German friends asked me ... to speak German so well.

4. "When shall we collect Joe at the airport?"
   We weren't sure ... at the airport.
5. "I'm so glad to see you again."
   When Peter saw Susan at the station he told her at once ... again.
6. "Please look after my flowers while we are on holiday in France."
   Our neighbour asked me ... while ... on holiday.
7. "How shall I answer these questions?"
   I don't know ...
8. "Mike and Mary have just left. But they he will be back soon." When I came to Mike's house his mother told me ... but that ... soon.
9. "Don't be late because the train will leave on time."
   The teacher told everybody ... because ... on time.
10. "I couldn't do this exercise."
    Jenny had to tell her teacher ... that exercise.

Übung 90: In der indirekten Rede wird das *simple present* beibehalten, wenn man betonen will, dass es sich um eine Gewohnheit, eine Eigenschaft oder ein Naturgesetz handelt. Übersetze:

1. Im Mittelalter *(the middle ages)* wollten die Leute einfach nicht glauben, dass die Erde nicht flach sei.
2. Herr Jackson war überrascht, dass seine Tochter Evelyne so gut Klavier spielt.
3. Pat erzählte uns, dass die Schule in Deutschland schon um 8 Uhr anfängt.
4. Sie erzählte uns auch, dass viele Deutsche nicht wussten, dass England und Großbritannien nicht dasselbe sind.
5. Sie sagte, dass die Städte, die sie letztes Jahr besucht habe, sehr berühmt seien.
6. Pat erzählte, dass die meisten Leute dort sehr gut Englisch sprechen.
7. Sie sagte, dass in den Bergen viele seltene Blumen wachsen.

Übung 91: Damit die indirekte Rede Sinn ergibt und der zeitliche oder örtliche Bezug eindeutig ist, müssen oft auch die Orts- und Zeitangaben geändert werden: *today/tonight → that day/night, this week/month → that week/month, yesterday / last Friday → the day / the Friday before, two days ago → two days before, tomorrow / next week → the next (following) day / week; here → there, in this town → in that town* (oder genaue Ortsangaben!)
Nun achte besonders auf die Orts- und Zeitangaben:

1. "Tomorrow I'm going to visit my son George in hospital."
   Three weeks ago Mr Raymond told me that ... in hospital ...
2. "He had an accident last week."
   He also said that his son ...
3. "A car ran into him just here in front of our house."
   He explained that a car ... just ... in front of ...
4. "George will come home this afternoon after he has been in hospital for three weeks."
   Last week I met Mr Raymond again and he told me that George ... after ...
5. "Last Friday we had dinner at Pierre's. This restaurant is excellent. We may go there again next Friday."
   I met them last Sunday and they told me that ... at Pierre's and that ... excellent. They said ...
6. "I can't help you today. Why didn't you ask me some days ago?"
   Last week I wanted George to help me renovating my room, but he said he ... and wanted to know why ...

Übung 92: Übersetze:

1. Ben sagte, dass er vielleicht am nächsten Tag zu uns kommen würde.
2. Bens Mutter sagte ihm, er solle erst seine Hausaufgaben machen.

3. Wir fragten ihn, warum er nicht mit dem Bus gekommen sei.
4. Jack hatte uns erzählt, dass er im nächsten Monat auf die Universität gehen wolle.
5. Peter sagt immer, dass er gerne Hockey spiele.
6. Niemand sagte ihm, dass sein Hund einige Stunden zuvor verletzt worden war.
7. Wir wussten nicht, wo wir die Karten kaufen sollten.
8. Mary hat uns nicht gesagt *(past tense)*, dass sie auch an dem Turnier teilnehmen wird.
9. Ihr Trainer hatte ihr gesagt, sie solle nichts sagen.

Übung 93: Entscheide, ob im Englischen ***when*** **(zeitliche Bedeutung)** oder ***if*** **(Bedingung)** stehen muss!

1. I'll give him the book if/when we have football training tomorrow evening.
2. What will you do if/when he comes to the party, too?
3. When/If I have a bad mark in English again I will get into trouble with my parents.
4. You'll surely improve your English if/when you go to Brighton next year.
5. I must show him the photos if/when I see him next time.
6. Don't tell her anything about the party if/when you happen to meet her.

Übung 94: Beschreibt der *if-Satz* eine **reale** (wirkliche, erfüllbare) Situation, können im *if-Satz* ***present tense*** oder ***present perfect*** und im Hauptsatz ***will-future***, **modale Hilfsverben** oder die **Befehlsform** stehen.
Unterstreiche die richtige Form:

1. If you go / you'll go to France, you must visit Paris.
2. I give / will give you the CD if I find / will find it.
3. You can buy the jeans if they aren't / won't be too expensive.
4. Peter doesn't show / won't show you the photos if you don't ask / won't ask him.
5. What do you say / will you say if he asks / will ask you to dance with him?
6. We can go to my place if my parents agree / will agree.
7. If she has found / will have found a new job, she may not be able to go on holiday with us.
8. We don't find / won't find out his new address if he has moved / will have moved to another town.

9. If Mike finds / will find a nice bike, he buys / will buy it at once.

Übung 95: Führe die folgenden Sätze mit den vorgegebenen Satzteilen fort:

1. We'll have dinner here if (restaurant/not expensive)
2. If you have learned enough you (pass/exam)
3. Don't tell him anything if (ask)
4. If you take the binoculars you (see/the castle)
5. Why haven't you invited him if (like)
6. If we want to be at the airport in time we (take/taxi)
7. If you think he's good enough for the team (give/chance)
8. If you ask him politely he (help)
9. Can I go to the station with you if (you/go by car)
10. If I have a good mark (I give/party)

Übung 96: Nun übersetze:

1. Wenn Pat uns wirklich besucht, müssen wir ihr die Sehenswürdigkeiten unserer Stadt zeigen.
2. Wenn du deine Hausaufgaben wieder nicht gemacht hast, wird Herr Mason deine Eltern informieren.
3. Wir werden mehr von der Landschaft sehen, wenn wir mit dem Fahrrad fahren.
4. Du kannst ihm nur helfen, wenn du mit ihm sprichst.
5. Du kannst viel Zeit sparen, wenn du deine Hausaufgaben ordentlich machst.
6. Wenn du schneller arbeitest, kannst du früher mit deinen Freunden spielen.
7. Wenn wir keine Lösung finden, werden wir viele Arbeiter entlassen *(to dismiss)* müssen.
8. Wenn Mary (noch) länger im Krankenhaus bleiben muss, wird sie noch mehr Probleme in der Schule bekommen.
9. Es wird leichter für sie sein, wenn wir ihr dann helfen.

10. Wirst du nach Birmingham fahren, wenn Peter dich einlädt, Susan?

Übung 97: Beschreiben *if-Satz* und *Hauptsatz* eine **Bedingung bzw. Folge**, die **in der Gegenwart oder Zukunft** erfüllt bzw. nicht erfüllt werden könnte, steht im *if-Satz* ***past tense*** und im *Hauptsatz* ***would/could/might + Infinitiv***. Das *simple past* von *to be* heißt hier immer *were*.
Setze die Verben in die richtige Zeit:

1. If they (try) harder, they might win the match.
2. We (not find) the way if we (not have) the map.
3. If I (not do) these odd jobs I (not afford) to go on holiday this year.
4. That wouldn't be a problem for me. If I (not can) go on holiday I (enjoy) the days here at home, too.
5. I (do) more sports, if I (not be) so busy.
6. If we (have) more time we might go to the theatre more often.
7. If Jack (be) at home, he (talk) to you. But he isn't!
8. Where (you/like) to live if you (have) the choice?
9. It (be) difficult to go shopping here if we (not have) the car.

Übung 98: Nun führe die Sätze selbständig fort. Beachte die vorgegebene Zeit!

1. I would really help you if (have/time)
2. If the weather is better, we (go/walk)
3. You could see better if (switch on/light)
4. If we had eggs and milk, we (can make/cake)
5. Would you lend him the money if (ask)
6. I would ring him up if (be/you)
7. I would do things differently if (be/own boss)
8. If she studies harder, she (be/better)
9. I couldn't give him any advice if he (ask)
10. You'll find the mistake if you (read/text/again)

Übung 99: Beantworte die Fragen mit den in Klammern vorgegebenen Satzteilen:

1. Will you invite Peter to the party?
   No. (If/do/have to invite Susan, too)
2. Will he take the exam next month?
   Yes. (If/not do/lose one year)
3. Will you post the letter this afternoon?
   Yes. (If/not do/Mike/not get it tomorrow)
4. Would you like to eat something?
   No. (If/do/not sleep/tonight)
5. Will you lend him your inline skates?
   No. (If/do/he/surely/have an accident)

Übung 100: Übersetze:

1. Wenn wir auf dem Land lebten *(in the country)*, würden wir unser eigenes Gemüse anbauen *(to grow)*.
2. Wenn er nicht geschäftlich unterwegs wäre *(away on business)*, könnte er mit uns ins Kino gehen.
3. Die Kinder könnten Schlittschuh laufen *(go skating)*, wenn der See gefroren wäre.
4. Wäre dein Bruder böse, wenn du sein Fahrrad nehmen würdest, ohne ihn zu fragen?
5. Wenn sie meine Kinder wären, dürften sie diesen Film nicht anschauen.
6. Wenn nicht so wenig Verkehr wäre, kämen wir nicht rechtzeitig zum Flughafen.
7. Wenn sie ihr Surfboard jetzt verkaufen würde, würde sie nicht viel Geld dafür bekommen.
8. Wenn wir morgen ins Kino gehen würden, könnten wir heute Tennis spielen.
9. Wenn du damit einverstanden wärst, würde ich die Karten kaufen.
10. Wir würden ihn sofort wiedererkennen, wenn er jetzt vor uns stehen würde.

Übung 101: Beschreiben *if-Satz* und *Hauptsatz* eine **Bedingung** bzw. **Folge**, die **in der Vergangenheit** hätte erfüllt bzw. nicht erfüllt werden können, steht im *if-Satz* ***past perfect*** und im *Hauptsatz* ***would/could/might + have + Infinitiv***. Setze die Verben in die richtigen Zeiten:

1. If we (catch) the bus, we (not miss) the start of the match.
2. If you (be) more careful, you (not break) all the glasses.
3. If Mary (study) the new words, she (get) a better mark.
4. We (leave) earlier if it (not rain).
5. If Peter (not go) to Birmingham he (might lose) his job.
6. (you/take) the job if they (offer) it to you?
7. I (hear) the phone if I (not take – progressive form!) a shower.
8. There (be) lots of problems if the school party (not be organized) so well.
9. If she (not operate on), she (might die)
10. If Pat (not be) to Germany several times, she (not get) this well-paid job.

Übung 102: Lies die vorgegebene Situation und bilde einen entsprechenden *if*-Satz:

1. He ran into the tree because he had drunk too much.
   If he ...
2. They were so thirsty because they had been running.
   If they ...
3. I was able to buy this bike because my parents paid a part of it.
   If my ...
4. She didn't buy the coat because it was too expensive.
   If the coat ...
5. We didn't tell him the truth because he was so weak.
   If he ...
6. Mrs Johnson didn't wake up her husband because he had arrived very late.
   If Mr Johnson ...

Übung 103: Übersetze:

1. Sie wäre mitgekommen, wenn sie nicht krank gewesen wäre.
2. Pat hätte nicht nach Deutschland fahren können, wenn sie nicht so gut Deutsch gelernt hätte.
3. Wenn Mike Peter nicht erinnert hätte, hätte er Susans Geburtstag vergessen.
4. Die Diebe hätten das ganze Haus ausgeraubt, wenn die Polizei nicht rechtzeitig gekommen wäre.
5. Aber wir hätten die Polizei nicht rufen können, wenn der Hund nicht gebellt hätte.
6. Was hättet ihr getan, wenn die Polizei nicht gekommen wäre?
7. Wenn der Wecker nicht geklingelt hätte, hätten wir verschlafen (to oversleep).
8. Wenn wir nicht solange geschlafen hätten, hätten wir den Sonnenaufgang gesehen.
9. Joe wäre nicht nach Amerika gegangen, wenn er hier eine Stelle gefunden hätte.
10. Wir hätten dieses Hotel nicht gefunden, wenn Peter es uns nicht empfohlen hätte (to recommend s.th. to s.b.).

Übung 104: Die zwei irrealen Typen der *if*-Sätze können auch vermischt werden, wenn es der Sinn erfordert. Unterstreiche die Verbform, die sinnvoll ist:

1. If I hadn't slept so long I wouldn't have to hurry now / I wouldn't have had to hurry now.
2. If she hadn't been in hospital for half a year, she could pass / would have been able to pass the exam next week.
3. We would have more fun now if you invited / had invited Peter, too.
4. He would never be happy again if he took / had taken the wrong decision last year.

5. If Peter hadn't practised so hard, the hockey coach would not let / would not have let him play in the next match.

Übung 105: Nun übersetze noch einmal – alle Möglichkeiten kommen vor:

1. Wir könnten dir helfen, wenn du uns rechtzeitig informiert hättest.
2. Frau Johnson wird sehr traurig sein, wenn sie ihre Wohnung verlassen muss.
3. Sie wäre erleichtert *(relieved)*, wenn sie wüsste, wo sie eine neue Wohnung finden könnte.
4. Sie hätte das Haus schon längst *(long ago)* fertig gestellt *(to finish)*, wenn sie genug Geld gehabt hätte.
5. Was würdet ihr tun, wenn ihr bei dem Preisausschreiben *(competition)* gewonnen hättet?
6. Wenn Jenny nicht zu Hause ist, wird sie bei ihrer Freundin sein.
7. Wenn er erfolgreicher gewesen wäre, hätte sie ihn geheiratet.
8. Aber ich frage mich, ob sie glücklich wären, wenn sie geheiratet hätten.
9. Ich würde diesen Pullover nicht kaufen, selbst wenn *(even if)* ich genug Geld hätte.
10. Wir könnten Tischtennis spielen, wenn er hierher kommen würde.

B. Tests

Test 1: *simple or progressive*

a) Entscheide, welche Form richtig ist:

1. Look, they are running / run after the dog.
2. Peter and Mike have been knowing / have known each other since their first school day.
3. I was reading / read my favourite book when the telephone rang / was ringing.
4. You should take an umbrella. It rains / is raining.
5. Last year we had / were having hockey training every Friday.
6. She has been talking / has talked to us for an hour now.
7. Next year we'll be laughing / will laugh about the problem we are having / have today.

b) Setze selbst die richtige Verbform ein. Du musst nun auch entscheiden, welche Zeit du brauchst:

1. ... (you/play) football when you ... (be) a child?
2. I ... (look) for my handbag for half an hour now. When I ... (see) it last it ... (lie) on the table.
3. Look, they ... (just/reach) the finishing-line.
4. You can't disturb them now. They ... (just/have) dinner.
5. Do you know that they ... (fly) to South Africa next month?
6. Yes, four weeks from today they ... (sit) in the plane.

c) Übersetze:

1. Ich konnte letzte Woche nicht ins Kino gehen. Ich habe mein Examen vorbereitet.
2. Zur Zeit spielen sie dieses Lied immer wieder.

3. Fred wohnt jetzt in London. Aber zur Zeit besucht er seine Eltern hier.
4. Er hat gestern versprochen anzurufen. Aber ich warte nun schon seit heute Vormittag auf seinen Anruf.
5. Wir warteten auf den Bus, als er uns ansprach.

Test 2: Zukunft

a) Welche der vorgegebenen Lösungen passt am besten in die Lücke?

1. I can't come on Saturday, I'm afraid. I ... my aunt then.
A. I'll see B. I see C. I'm seeing

2. I'm so thirsty. – Wait I ... a glass of water for you.
A. I'm fetching B. I'll fetch C. I'm going to fetch

3. She has just told me that they ... .
A. will marry B. marry C. are going to marry

4. We must leave now. The train ... at 13.35
A. leaves B. will leave C. is going to leave

5. They think that they ... into their new house at Easter.
A. are going to move B. move C. will move

6. We ... our living room next Saturday.
A. will renovate B. are renovating C. renovate

7. Would you like some tea? – Yes, ... a cup.
A. I'll take B. I'm taking C. I'm going to take

b) Übersetze:

1. Weißt du, wann der Zug morgen fährt?
2. Wirst du sie morgen sehen? – Nein, ich werde morgen mein Fahrrad reparieren.

3. Hast du die Eintrittskarten? – Oh, nein. Ich hole sie sofort.
4. Was machst du heute abend? – Ich gehe mit Freunden ins Kino.
5. Ich glaube, dass der Film euch gefallen wird. Ich werde ihn nächstes Wochenende auch anschauen.
6. Ich fahre nächsten Samstag nach Paris.

Test 3: *present tense – present perfect*

a) Entscheide, welche Form richtig ist:

1. I can't believe that he's a criminal. I know / have known him so well.
2. Peter is / has been ill. He is lying / has been lying in bed since Friday.
3. Where is he / has he been? I don't see / haven't seen him for two hours.
4. I know / have known everything about the accident. He tells / has told me the whole story.
5. How long are you working / have you been working here?
6. It's terrible. Kate simply doesn't talk / hasn't talked to me – although we always understand / have always understood each other so well.

b) Nun setze selbständig die richtige Form ein. Du musst auch zwischen *simple* und *progressive form* entscheiden.

1. She ... (win) the competiton. But she ... (practise) very hard for this victory.
2. Mrs Newton ... (show) her family photos to everybody. Nobody ... (ever succeed) in avoiding to look at them.
3. I ... (look) for the newspaper since breakfast and you ... (read) it.
4. Ann ... (lose) her job. Now she ... (try) to find a new one.
5. Your car ... (break down)? Why ... (you/not buy) a new one?

c) Übersetze:

1. Ich rauche seit zwei Monaten nicht mehr.
2. Seit wann hast du den Führerschein *(driver's licence)*?
3. Wir fahren immer mit dem Bus. Aber heute haben wir ihn verpasst.
4. Sie wohnen schon immer nebeneinander. Aber jetzt streiten sie.

Test 4: *present perfect – past tense – past perfect*

a) Bilde vollständige Sätze:

1. I/not smoke/since/doctor/tell/me/to stop/it
2. yesterday/he/promise to come/but/he/not appear/yet
3. we/order/a bottle of champagne/after/he/pass/his exam
4. Mary/not know/if/Mike/be injured/in the accident/too
5. since/I/buy/the book/I/read/it/three times
6. they/promise/to deliver*(liefern)*/the cupboard/in time/but/ we/only/get/it/yesterday
7. I/ask/Peter/to help me/to repair my bike/because/he/ already/repair/his own one

b) Nun finde selbst die richtige Lösung:

1. I ... (be) so pleased to see her again after we ... (not see) each other for years.
2. He ... (open) the letter and then ... (sit down) to answer it at once.
3. He doesn't want to tell me where he ... (buy) this shirt.
4. The dress is damaged? Why ... (you/not bring) it back yet?
5. The house ... (be) completely quiet when I ... (return) because everybody ... (already/go) to bed.
6. Sorry I ... (miss) the overture (Ouverture). But the bus ... (break down) on the way here.

c) Übersetze:

1. Tom war schon fortgegangen, als ich bei ihm ankam. Er hatte ein Taxi genommen.
2. Seit wann weißt du, dass sie in Paris geheiratet haben?
3. Sie benahm sich *(to behave)*, als ob sie ihn nie zuvor gesehen hätte.
4. Wir fragen uns schon lange, ob sie damals *(then)* die richtige Entscheidung getroffen haben.

Test 5: Modale Hilfsverben

a) Welche der Lösungen passt am besten in die Lücke?

1. Last year he lost his job but he ... find a new one very soon.
   A. can B. could c. was able to

2. The restaurant was excellent. We ... choose between five different desserts.
   A. were able to B. could C. might

3. Be careful! The teacher ... ask you some old words, too.
   A. may B. must C. will be able to

4. Please go outside, Sir. You ... smoke in here.
   A. mustn't B. can't C. aren't allowed to

5. ... I give you some advice, Miss? – Oh, yes. I really need one.
   A. May B. Can C. Should

6. She looks so sad. Do you think we ... talk to her?
   A. can B. should C. might

7. Don't you see I'm working. You ... always disturb me.
   A. needn't B. shouldn't C. mustn't

8. It's only a suggestion. You ... accept it if you don't want.
   A. musnt't B. needn't C. aren't allowed to

b) Übersetze:

1. Wir mussten sehr schwierige Fragen beantworten.
2. Nur wenige sollen den Test bestanden haben.
3. Peter brauchte nicht bis zum Schluss bleiben, er durfte früher gehen.
4. Ihr solltet die Bücher gestern schon mitbringen.
5. Ihr müsst euch deswegen keine Sorgen machen.

Test 6: Passiv

a) In jedem Satz ist ein Fehler. Finde und korrigiere ihn.

1. The dog has being looked for since breakfast.
2. The new museum is opened next year.
3. Look, the doors are just been opened.
4. Their new CD has been published last week.
5. The car must being repaired at once.
6. The box should been opened carefully.
7. The windows are cleaned every week from Chris.
8. The criminal was been observed for four weeks.
9. The cat couldn't be find anywhere.

b) Bilde vollständige Sätze im Passiv. Entscheide, welche Zeit du verwenden musst:

1. new cinema/open/tomorrow evening
2. The newspaper said that (nobody/injure/in the accident)
3. The injured girl couldn't walk and (must take/to hospital/ambulance men)
4. missing child/not find/yet/police

5. witnesses *(Zeugen)*/question/for over two hours now
6. My bike is gone (it/must/steal)
7. You needn't give a tip *(Trinkgeld)*. (service/include/in the bill)
8. (exhibition/still/prepare) when the famous artist arrived.
9. I'm sure that (decision/not take/before next week)
10. It was a difficult campaign *(Wahlkampf)* but (in the end/he/elect/president)

c) Übersetze und verwende dabei das Passiv:

1. Man wird diesen Baum fällen müssen.
2. Man hat die Straße vor einem Jahr gebaut.
3. Seit wann nennt man sie Billy?
4. Die Bürgermeisterin selbst dankte den Kindern für ihre Aufmerksamkeit.
5. Man wird uns sehr viele Fragen stellen.
6. Die Verkäuferin zeigte ihr verschiedene Kleider.

Test 7: Indirekte Rede

a) Finde den Fehler und korrigiere:

1. Did you know that his father has been in hospital for three weeks?
2. Mrs Walters told me that he will come home again next week.
3. Why didn't you ask your teammate if he already saw the film.
4. They wanted to know what we were doing when the accident happened.
5. I had to admit *(zugeben)* that I haven't been practising enough piano recently *(in letzter Zeit)*.
6. I already knew that he is in town again.
7. Did they tell the police where they hid the money?
8. Why didn't they ask me where they can find the basketball?

b) Setze in die indirekte Rede:

1. "I don't think that this colour suits you."
   Rob told his girlfriend that ...
2. "Peter will help us tomorrow."
   Peter had promised her that ...
3. "Don't wait with your visit until next week."
   My mum had told me ...
4. "He doesn't like this sort of cake."
   I warned her that ...
5. "I hope that I can go to Germany next year."
   Susan told me ...

c) Bilde die indirekten Fragen:

1. "Where can we find the petrol station?"
   We didn't know ...
2. "How shall I do this exercise?"
   Nellie asked her teacher ...
3. "Where are the trousers that you bought yesterday?"
   Peter's mother wanted to know ...
4. "By when must we have finished the German paper?"
   The pupils weren't sure ...
5. "Who told you that lie?"
   John asked me ...

Test 8: If-Sätze

a) Die folgenden Sätze geben keinen Sinn. Wie müssen sie richtig heißen? Verbessere die unterstrichenen Satzteile:

1. If you ask him this question, he wouldn't answer.
2. I would sleep long if I don't have to work today.
3. We would get better seats if we had arrived earlier.

4. Sally might have won the race if she didn't stumble *(stolpern)*.
5. Mary could get into trouble if she doesn't start to concentrate on school.
6. Don't answer the phone even if it kept ringing.
7. Will you join a cooking club if they founded one?
8. He wouldn't have been so happy today if he hadn't met this wonderful girl.
9. If she had the possibility when she was young she would have travelled around the world.
10. I would really help you if I can.

b) Setze die richtige Form ein:

1. If I ... (be) Henry, I would accept this offer at once.
2. Would you ask your friends to borrow you some money if you ... (need) it for a CD?
3. If he gives up smoking now his health ... (improve).
4. If it ... (not be) raining we could have lunch in the garden.
5. We ... (organize) a party if we had known that it was his birthday today.
6. If more than hundred people ... (come) to the concert tomorrow it will be a success.
7. Mr Miller ... (not be) angry if you hadn't broken his window.
8. I wouldn't take the bus today if it ... (not rain).
9. Would you have promised to help her if you ... (know) what her problem was?
10. She ... (understand) it if you explained it to her.

Lösungen

Teil A

Übung 1:

1. Mary always watches the cartoons on Channel 4.
2. She doesn't like German lessons.
3. She doesn't do her homework carefully.
4. She plays the guitar quite well.
5. Does Bob live in the green house in Mansion Road?
6. Is he a member of the hockey team?
7. He plays hockey.
8. He doesn't like football.

Übung 2:

zum Beispiel: At first I turn off the alarm clock. Then I get up and open the curtains. I wash myself / take a shower, brush my teeth and comb my hair. Then I have breakfast and read the newspaper. Sometimes I do the rest of my homework. Finally I leave for school. Usually I run for the bus.

Übung 3:

is sitting, isn't doing, is looking, is raining, is carrying, Is Mary dreaming, is smiling

Übung 4:

Die Signalwörter sind: every day, often, At the moment, always, Usually, Right now, never

1. Mike and Mary see each other every day.
2. Pat often writes letters to her German pen friend.
3. At the moment she is listening to a CD with German songs.
4. She doesn't always understand the lyrics.
5. Usually she looks up the unknown words in her dictionary.
6. Right now she is looking for a word she doesn't know.
7. Susan never sleeps long on Sunday mornings.

Übung 5:

richtig ist:

1. lives, is working 2. is baking, invites 3. often rains 4. go 5. are singing, buy 6. is talking, calls 7. are you looking, lie

Übung 6:

1. is coming 2. is mowing 3. mows, does 4. is testing, isn't working, is still making

Übung 7:

1. hates, watch 2. wants, isn't listening, sees, is going on 3. likes, calls, is trying, hears, are playing, knows 4. is waiting, know, am looking, Do you remember 5. has, are visiting *(nur solange er im Krankenhaus ist!)* 6. don't need, have, are wearing

Übung 8:

switches on, begins, stops, are waiting, hears, fetches, jumps, are watching, disappears

Übung 9:

1. I can't answer the phone. I'm (just) taking a shower.
2. Peter goes to the cinema two or three times every month.
3. Mike wants to buy a new mountain bike. So he's saving his pocket money.
4. When the doors open hundreds of fans are already waiting in front of the concert hall.
5. I'm not sure if he's already sleeping. Probably he's listening to his CDs.
6. Do you remember Jane? She looks like Madonna.
7. Where does your friend live? – He lives in London. But at the moment he is staying with his uncle in Birmingham.
8. Usually he always tells jokes. But today he feels bad.
9. Mostly the sun shines here. What a pity that it's raining today. But nevertheless we're having much fun together.
10. Listen! The dog is barking. He hears that Bob is coming home. Bob goes for a walk with him every evening.

Übung 10:

1. Do you know, will go 2. doesn't work, hopes, will get 3. attends, won't see 4. wants, will find 5. will write, am, won't be able to, will explain, want

Übung 11:

1. He knows him quite well.
2. The suitcase is too heavy for you. Wait, I'll help you.
3. The concert will last two hours. That means that we won't be back before 11 p.m.
4. He'll surely be tired when he arrives.
5. I'm quite sure that Peter will lose the match. He plays tennis badly.
6. I'll call you tomorrow morning, o.k.?
7. I'll read the letter as soon as I get it.
8. Let's go shopping. The shops will close soon.

Übung 12:

1. Peter will be working at 9 a.m.
2. The band will be playing until midnight.
3. The sun will be shining tomorrow.
4. Julia will be waiting when we arrive.
5. The children will be sleeping when grandma calls.
6. Susan will be laughing when she hears this.

1. Will Peter be working at 9 a.m.?
2. The band won't be playing until midnight.
3. Will the sun be shining tomorrow?
4. Will Julia be waiting when we arrive?
5. The children won't be sleeping when grandma calls.
6. Susan won't be laughing when she hears this.

Übung 13:

1. will be lying, will be, will be having, won't be doing, won't come, will be watching, will be listening
2. will know, will be reading, will be talking, won't look, will be dreaming

Übung 14:

will have developed, will have started, will have lost, will have caught a cold, I won't have forgotten, will have written, Will Tony have forgotten

Übung 15:

1. will be waiting ... until 2. will have finished ... by 3. will have known 4. will be celebrating 5. By ... will have passed 6. Will you have finished ... by 7. won't be suffering, will have recovered ... by, will be playing

Übung 16:

1. When does the theatre begin? – It begins at 8 p.m.
2. What day is tomorrow? – Tomorrow is Tuesday.
3. When does the next English course start? – It starts in September.
4. When does your football training end this evening? – It ends at 6.30 p.m.
5. When do the holidays start this year? – They start on August 1st.
6. Where do we meet the guide? – We meet him in front of the hotel.

Übung 17:

1. How long are you staying?
2. When are you leaving?
3. Are you going alone?
4. Are you going by train?
5. Are you staying at a youth hostel?
6. Where are you going first?
7. Are you taking a diving course?

1. I'm staying for two weeks.
2. I'm leaving on Thursday.
3. No, I'm going with Mary.
4. Yes, we're going by train.
5. No, we're staying at a camping site.
6. First we are going to the coast.
7. No, we are not taking a diving course.

Übung 18:

1. are going, does it start 2. is working 3. Are you coming, starts 4. start, I'm not going out 5. are playing, does the game start

Übung 19:

zum Beispiel: I'm going to visit friends / I'm going (to go) to the cinema / I'm going to play tennis / I'm going to sleep long / I'm going to meet my friends at the disco ...

Übung 20:
Richtig ist:
1. is going to buy, will be 2. is going to paint, will be 3. is going to have, will have 4. won't rain, is going to celebrate 5. will write, I'm going to study 6. I'll ask

Übung 21:
1. Bob and Mike are going for a biking tour this afternoon. Are you coming too, Mary? – I'm afraid I must learn. I'll be sitting at my desk while you are having fun.
2. I've missed the bus, Mum. Now I'll be late at school. When I arrive, the lesson will already have started and the teacher will be controlling the homework. – Ok, I'll take you there by car.
3. Have you seen the poster, Mike? Our favourite band is coming next month. – I know. I'm going to buy a ticket tomorrow. – Good idea. I'll come with you.
4. How will we get to the stadium? – By bus. It leaves at 18.33. We must be there on time. Otherwise we'll miss the concert.

Übung 22:
was, broke, cut, lay, said, began, bought, drove, left, paid, spoke, ate, gave, knew, taught, threw, found, heard, thought, wrote

Übung 23:
1. Did you watch the film on TV yesterday evening?
2. I saw the accident.
3. Pat didn't do German at school.
4. Mike got up early this morning.
5. Did Peter play the tennis match yesterday?
6. Yes, but he didn't win.

Übung 24:
came, went, opened, looked, was, took, read, was, read, thought, sat, started

Übung 25:
1. Mike was riding his mountain bike.
2. Pat was studying for her German course.
3. Mike and Mary were planning their holidays.
4. Bob was going for a walk with his dog.
5. Susan was writing a letter to Peter.
6. Peter was watching TV with his uncle.

Übung 26:
1. Was Mike riding his mountain bike?
2. Was Pat studying for her German course?
3. Were Mike and Mary planning their holidays?
4. Bob wasn't going for a walk with his dog.
5. Susan wasn't writing a letter to Peter.
6. Peter wasn't watching TV with his uncle.

Übung 27:

1. were sitting, started, ran 2. were talking, were watching 3. Was John driving, happened 4. was waiting, arrived, brought 5. were dancing, didn't want, was only thinking 6. saw, was going 7. was working, met 8. were just having, brought

Übung 28:

It was Friday evening. Mrs Miller was preparing supper, when she heard the noise. She wanted to call her husband, but he was repairing the car in the garage.
Mrs Miller left the kitchen and went into the living room. While she was looking out of the window, she saw a man who was running towards the house. He was carrying something in his arms. Then he knocked on the door.
While Mrs Miller was thinking what to do the man shouted: "Open the door, please. This dog is bleeding heavily." Mrs Miller opened the door and said: „Come in. You are lucky. My husband is a vet."
And while Mrs Miller was getting her husband, the man put the dog on the table. While Mr Miller was examining the dog, his wife was looking for a phone number on the dog licence disc. The owner was already missing the dog when Mrs Miller called him. He was glad when he heard that Mr Miller was able to save his dog.

Übung 29:

1. Bob has closed the window.
2. John hasn't cleaned his shoes.
3. Has it stopped raining?
4. We haven't seen the film.
5. Mike has found his keys.
6. Has Susan bought some bread?
7. Peter hasn't called Susan yet.
8. Mary has washed the dishes.
9. She has gone shopping.
10. Have you been to the hairdresser's?

Übung 30:

1. Have you met him yet? (in der Frage heißt „schon" *yet!)*
2. He has always smoked these expensive cigars.
3. Have you ever been to America?
4. I haven't washed the car yet this month.
5. They have never been friends.
6. I haven't found the solution yet.
7. We've just come home.
8. Have you done your homework yet?
9. They have always gone to the station by taxi.
10. Joe has never lived in London.

Übung 31:

1. has been, for, has felt, since 2. has played, since 3. hasn't come, for 4. has wanted, for 5. has planned, for 6. has already read 7. have known, since 8. has liked, since

Übung 32:

1. didn't see, visited 2. Have you seen *(this week* ist kein fester Zeitpunkt in der Vergangenheit, sondern hat eine ähnliche Bedeutung wie *bis heute)* 3. haven't finished, finished 4. became 5. Have you ever gone, went 6. have opened, did they open 7. did you buy (auch *where* ist eine Ortsangabe), got 8. played, have never heard 9. has just left, called 10. did they go, didn't ask, left

Übung 33:

1. saw 2. have wanted, started, have never had 3. have saved, spent, were, have become, has met, started 4. has promised, have got, was

Übung 34:

1. How long have you been waiting? – I've been waiting for one minute.
2. How long has the sun been shining? – It has been shining since this morning.
3. How long has the baby been crying? – It has been crying since midnight.
4. How long has Pat been learning German? – She has been learning German for a long time.
5. How long have you been listening to the radio? – I have been listening to the radio since I woke up this morning.
6. How long have Bob and Mike been jogging? They have been jogging for one hour.

Übung 35:

1. Pat has been writing to her German penfriend for one hour.
2. Bob has been playing with his dog since this afternoon.
3. We have been waiting for the bus to the football stadium for half an hour.
4. Mike and Mary have been planning their holidays in Germany for weeks.
5. Peter has been looking for his purse since he came back from school.
6. Since the train's departure Jenny has been standing.
7. You have been eating chocolate for hours.
8. I have been looking forward to your visit for days.

Übung 36:

1. have been hitch-hiking, for hours, haven't got 2. haven't been waiting, has just arrived 3. have been playing, since breakfast 4. have been looking, for half an hour, haven't seen 5. has been mowing, since, hasn't finished 6. Has Mike done, has been talking, since lunch 7. haven't heard, since 8. has been lying, since Sunday, hasn't got

Übung 37:

1. When Pat was living in the country she didn't go out very often in the evenings. Now she has lived / has been living in London for one year, she has often gone to the disco and she has attended a German course.
2. Have you already seen the new film? – Yes, I saw it with Mike last week.
3. Since when has Pat been able to speak German so well? – She worked as an au pair in Munich last summer.
4. I've never heard such a great CD. Peter was listening to it, too, when I was talking to him on the phone. – I know. He gave it to me for my birthday.

5. Peter has had a new girl friend for three weeks. – That's not true. When I was at the cinema yesterday, he was sitting behind me with Susan.
6. We've had bad weather for two weeks now. Last year the summer was beautiful. The sun was shining almost the whole time.
7. Why didn't Mike want to come to the party last Friday? – He has been quarrelling with Mary for three weeks.
8. I've just baked a cake. Would you like a piece? – Thank you, I haven't eaten anything for hours.
9. Since when has he been at our school? – I don't know. I've just seen him for the first time, too. But he has been looking at us all the time.

Übung 38:

1. Als er den Brief gelesen hatte 2. nachdem er nach Hause gekommen war 3. obwohl sie sich das Bein gebrochen hatte 4. als er uns alles erzählt hatte 5. Nachdem wir eine Stunde lang gesucht hatten 6. weil sie viel Geld gewonnen hatte 7. was sich auf der Party ereignet hatte

Übung 39:

1. He called Susan after he had arrived at Birmingham.
2. Mike was late for school because he had missed the bus.
3. Mary didn't go on the biking tour because she had broken her leg.
4. I bought this CD after I had been to the concert.
5. I fell in love with Mike after we had danced at the party.
6. I didn't write you a postcard because I had forgotten your address.
7. He didn't go by car because he had lost his keys.
8. Pat went to Germany after she had found a nice family.

Übung 40:

1. Susan went to Birmingham because Peter had invited her.
2. Mike bought a new saddle for his bike after his father had given him the money.
3. After it had been sunny for two weeks it started to rain.
4. Mike finally got the CD after he had been in three shops.
5. Pat was happy because Tony had sent her a photo of himself.
6. The burglar ran away because the alarm had started to ring.
7. Bob's dog Ronny came after Bob had called him three times.
8. They visited Mary in hospital because she had broken her leg.

Übung 41:

1. called, had fetched 2. had, had been 3. didn't forget, had returned 4. had liked, met 5. called, had heard 6. found out, had only been 7. didn't come, had invited 8. wanted, had lost

Übung 42:

1. had been watching, switched off 2. had been learning, said 3. had opened, came 4. had been walking 5. visited, had read 6. had been shining, started 7. had you been looking, found 8. had known, liked 9. had been running, had heard 10. had almost given up, arrived

Übung 43:

1. had just come back, called, had been trying
2. came, had already been looking, wanted
3. had been painting, was, got into bed
4. came, were waiting, had organized
5. had already been playing hockey, arrived, had had
6. was doing, remembered, had promised, had been talking

Übung 44:

1. We had been walking for three hours when it started to rain.
2. We knew Joe quite well because we had often played with him.
3. After the trainer had observed Peter for a while he was allowed to play on the team.
4. Pat was talking all the time about the boy she had met during her holidays.
5. At the end of the school excursion Bob's teacher was looking for some boys. But they had already got on the bus.
6. The children were tired. They had been outdoors all day.
7. She couldn't believe that she had succeeded in passing the test.

Übung 45:

1. I will be able to help you.
2. We haven't been able to help them.
3. Mary was able to play volleyball again.
4. The Walters weren't able to find a new house.
5. I haven't been able to come to your party.
6. Will they be able to come?
7. Pat hasn't been able to sleep well.
8. Was she able to do her homework?
9. We won't be able to open the shop in time.
10. The driver had been able to stop in front of the child.

Übung 46:

1. could, was able to 2. were able to 3. could 4. was able to 5. was able to 6. was able to 7. could 8. could, was able to

Übung 47:

1. I can't bring, Could you fetch 2. Could you take, She can't walk 3. we could only choose 4. Peter could go 5. We could speak 6. Can you explain 7. We could see 8. We can show 9. I could come 10. Could she call

Übung 48:

1. After Pat had attended the German course she was able to understand her German pen friend much better.
2. So far we haven't been able to go abroad.
3. But next year we will be able to afford a holiday in France.
4. Last year we could visit some interesting French cities on a coach tour. I could give you some information.

5. But we couldn't visit all the sights. Time was too short.
6. Mary was able to pass the math exam last week. The pupils could choose between different tasks.
7. I have't been able to reach him yet. Could you give me his new phone number?
8. Pat will soon be able to see Tony again. He was able to persuade his boss to let him go to London.
9. We haven't been able to find a solution so far. I hope we will be able to give you a positive answer soon.

Übung 49:

1. He may/might be right.
2. Bob may/might have missed the bus.
3. We may/might see him next month.
4. He may/might have met him.
5. Joe may/might write soon.
6. Mary may/might have wanted to come, too.
7. They may/might not marry.
8. We may/might find a solution.

Übung 50:

1. Peter will be allowed to go swimming ...
   Peter has been allowed to go swimming ...
   Peter was allowed to go swimming ...
2. Mary won't be allowed to do so much sport ...
   Mary wasn't allowed to do so much sport ...
   Mary hasn't been allowed to do so much sport ...

Übung 51:

1. May I invite you to dinner? – Yes, you may.
2. May Susan come this evening? – No, she may not.
3. May we show you the city? – Of course, you may.
4. May I use your car? – No, you may not.
5. May we come later this evening? – No, you may not.
6. May I buy this book? – Yes, you may.

Übung 52:

1. vielleicht (könnte ... sein) 2. darfst 3. darfst nicht 4. kennt vielleicht nicht. 5. vielleicht 6. darf 7. darf 8. vielleicht

Übung 53:

1. are allowed, mustn't 2. aren't allowed 3. can, aren't allowed 4. aren't allowed 5. can, mustn't, aren't allowed 6. Can we have, is allowed

Übung 54:

1. May 2. will be allowed to 3. mustn't 4. can 5. wasn't allowed 6. May we go, may not 7. has been allowed to

Übung 55:

1. Susan wasn't allowed to come to Peter's Party because she was ill.
2. May I take a piece of cake? – Of course you may. Help yourself.
3. We can talk about everything, but you mustn't lie to me.
4. You aren't allowed to read the magazines if you don't want to buy them.
5. Mrs Johnson has been in hospital for three days and we haven't been allowed to visit her yet.
6. Do you think you will be allowed to go on holiday with Mike. – I hope I will be able to persuade my parents.
7. In Britain pupils aren't allowed to wear the clothes they want at school.
8. May I sit down here? – I'm afraid (you may) not. The seat is taken.
9. No, you mustn't go to the cinema with your brother. Children under 16 aren't allowed to see that film.

Übung 56:

1. needn't 2. must 3. needn't 4. needn't, must 5. needn't 6. must

Übung 57:

1. You won't have to wash the dishes.
2. You had to come back on time.
3. We haven't had to use the first aid box.
4. You didn't have to help me. You had to clean up your room.
5. Mike didn't have to look at his mother.
6. Susan will have to do her homework.

Übung 58:

1. didn't have to 2. Will we have to 3. had to 4. needn't 5. have had to 6. Did you have to, didn't have to 7. needn't look, will have to 8. has had to

Übung 59:

1. mustn't 2. needn't 3. needn't 4. mustn't 5. mustn't 6. needn't

Übung 60:

Richtig ist: 1. have to 2. must 3. must 4. have to 5. must 6. has to

Übung 61:

1. You needn't switch on the heating. It's warm enough in here.
2. Last week Bob had to go to the vet with his dog.
3. The concert ends at midnight. We'll have to collect the children by car.
4. My father is waiting. I have to go. – That's a pity. But you must taste a piece of cake. You mustn't go without.
5. My parents are very strict. I'll have to stay at home on Sunday.
6. The service in the restaurant was very good. We didn't have to wait long for our meal.
7. You needn't buy the tickets. I'll be able to get them.
8. Did we have to do any maths homework? – Of course, we did. But you needn't copy them any more, the teacher is coming.

9. The house is quite old. We will have to renovate everything. – You needn't worry about that. Our friends will help us.
10. I needn't get up so early today because it is Saturday.
11. You have to leave the cat outside because of the people who are allergic to cats.

Übung 62:

1. are to, Shall 2. is said to 3. should / ought to 4. shall 5. should / ought to 6. is said to 7. were to 8. Shall, are to 9. mustn't 10. shouldn't / ought not to

Übung 63:

1. You shouldn't watch TV so long, Peter.
2. Where shall we put the piano?
3. Where is Mike? He was to be here half an hour ago. We should / ought to call him.
4. Bob's dog is said to have bitten him. Is that true? – Nonsense. You should see Ronny. He's a good dog.
5. Which blouse shall I take? – No idea. But hurry up. We are to be home at three.
6. You shouldn't / ought not to wait so long with your answer. He's said to become impatient very fast.
7. You must start / Start with your homework now. You are to know the words tomorrow.
8. Do you know what has happened to Joe? – He's said to live in New York now.
9. You should always ask your teacher if you are to write down the sentences, too.

Übung 64:

1. The photo was made last year.
2. The song is played quite often on the radio.
3. New information has just been given.
4. A lot of people had been invited to the party.
5. Their new CD will be published next month.
6. The car can be repaired.
7. The ambulance has been called.
8. The problem will be solved soon.

Übung 65:

1. When was the photo made?
2. The song isn't played quite often on the radio.
3. Has new information been given?
4. Had a lot of people been invited?
5. Their new CD won't be published next month.
6. The car can't be repaired.
7. Has the ambulance been called?
8. Will the problem be solved soon?

Übung 66:

1. The exhibition is being opened.
2. The little dog was being punished.
3. Are the windows being cleaned?

4. Was the wall being painted?
5. Is the dog being taken for a walk?
6. The injured man is being helped.
7. The stew is beeing cooked.
8. The film was being shown in the assembly hall.

Übung 67:

Der Handlungsverursacher ist wichtig in den Sätzen 2, 5, 6, 8, 11 und 12.

Übung 68:

1. Tickets aren't sold before the concert.
2. Was the new boy invited to the party by Mary?
3. Will the school building be renovated?
4. Ronny's dog hasn't been found yet.
5. The exhibition had been visited by thousands of people before it closed.
6. The ambulance was called by a little boy.
7. The surprise party has been planned very carefully.
8. The accident was caused by a big lorry.
9. Can your car be repaired?
10. The shop was just being closed when I arrived.
11. He was informed about his winnings in the lottery by a letter.
12. Was the concert organized by Peter?

Übung 69:

2. Wurde von Mary der neue Junge zur Party eingeladen?
5. Die Austellung war von Tausenden von Menschen besucht worden, bevor sie schloss.
6. Der Krankenwagen ist von einem kleinen Jungen gerufen worden.
8. Der Unfall ist durch einen großen Lkw verursacht worden.
11. Er ist durch einen Brief über seinen Lottogewinn informiert worden.
12. Ist das Konzert von Peter organisiert worden?

Übung 70:

1. Will the school be renovated soon?
2. This question is often asked by the parents.
3. We will start during the next holidays.
4. The pupils will help.
5. The classrooms will be painted by the pupils.
6. The parents will be informed exactly by a letter.
7. Donations are already needed this month.
8. A bank account is just being opened.
9. The renovation will also be supported by the newspaper.
10. The new roof will be paid by the town council.

Übung 71:

1. Bob was woken up by the dog last night.

2. The burglar had been chased away by the dog.
3. New locks will be put in tomorrow.
4. The heating must be turned on.
5. The injured boy is being looked after by a nurse.
6. Must he be operated on the arm?

Übung 72:

1. Peter had been sent to Birmingham by his boss.
2. Susan hopes that she will be rang up by Peter soon.
3. The forms have already been filled in.
4. The shoes must be taken off.
5. These beautiful old trees have been cut down.
6. You know that the money must be paid back.
7. These papers mustn't be thrown away.
8. The thief was shot down by the police.
9. The cat was run over by a drunken driver.
10. The accident will be reported on in the local newspaper.

Übung 73:

1. We are just being shown some holiday photos by Mary.
2. Peter is paid more money by the company because he has gone to Birmingham.
3. Pat will be sent the au pair family's address next week.
   The au pair familiy's address will be sent to Pat next week.
4. She had already been sent a lot of useful information about her stay in Germany.
   A lot of useful information about her stay in Germany had already been sent to her.
5. She was being asked a lot of questions in the interview by the members of the committee.
6. Mike was given the rest of the money for his mountain bike by his parents.
   The rest of the money for his mountain bike was given to Mike by his parents.
7. Joe's friends have been sent these photos of New York by Joe himself.
   These photos of New York have been sent to Joe's friends by Joe himself.

Übung 74:

1. He is just being brought home.
2. Mary was operated on the leg yesterday.
3. Mike has been elected team captain.
4. All inhabitants will be invited.
5. All residents are being asked/questioned if they have seen the burglar.
6. The burglar will be found.
7. The new shopping centre will be opened tomorrow.
8. All the old houses have been renovated.

Übung 75:

1. Mary zeigt uns gerade einige Urlaubsphotos.
2. Man wird Pat die neue Adresse nächste Woche schicken.
3. Man hatte ihr bereits viele nützliche Informationen geschickt.

4. Die Mitglieder des Komitees haben ihr viele Fragen gestellt.
5. Mikes Eltern habe ihm das restliche Geld gegeben.
6. Joe selbst hat seinen Freunden diese Photos geschickt.

Übung 76:

1. Mike was offered a used mountain bike yesterday.
   A used mountain bike was offered to Mike yesterday.
2. At the tourist information Pat was shown the way to the station on the map.
3. This story was always read to me by my grandmother.
4. Mike has been promised £3 by the neighbour, if he mows her lawn.
5. The helpers were thanked by the rescued tourists.
6. The drinks have already been paid for by this gentleman.
7. The whole beach has been polluted by oil.
8. Joe is said to live in New York now.
9. She has been promised that she will be back at home in two weeks time.
10. They will be shown how they can protect themselves.
11. After the opening the minister was thanked for his speech.
12. When Mary came home from hospital, she was helped a lot at school.

Übung 77:

1. The new cinema will be opened next week.
2. Mike has already been given ...
3. The exercise was explained to us by our teacher.
4. At the moment the dog is being fed by Ronny.
5. The soup must be taken off ...
6. A lot of houses were damaged by the storm.
7. The heating has been turned on.
8. The woman could be saved.
9. The doors are just being opened.

Übung 78:

1. she can't find her purse and that she must have lost it.
2. she can't come to her birthday party.
3. her friend doesn't like dancing.
4. she saw you at the youth club with your new girlfriend.
5. I've already brought your CD back.
6. I'll miss a great concert if I don't come with you.
7. you don't want to see me again.

Übung 79:

1. when you are leaving for Dresden.
2. where she bought that sweatshirt.
3. if she has known him long.
4. if we are to do the English homework for tomorrow.
5. where Peter works?
6. how much you paid for the bike?

7. why I didn't come to the hockey match.
8. what the time is, please.
9. if/whether we will find the way to their house.
10. when I left my house.

Übung 80:
folgende Fragen können verkürzt werden: 1, 4, 6, 7, 8

Übung 81:
1. when to meet him this evening.
4. where to find a suitable flat.
6. how to explain this to Peter.
7. whether to tell him the truth.
8. why to explain anything to him.

Übung 82:
1. I wonder when to write this letter.
2. He would like to know when to be at the station.
3. She doesn't know if/whether her bike can be repaired.
4. Can you tell me where my trousers are?
5. I don't know how to help you.
6. Everybody asks me when the party will start.
7. I don't know whether you are to answer this question.
8. Please tell me when to call you.
9. I'm not sure if/whether he'll come, too.
10. I wonder why you are here.

Übung 83:
1. Lasst uns ihn fragen, wann wir ihn am Flughafen abholen sollen.
2. Sie weiß nicht, ob sie einen Mantel anziehen soll.
3. John hat mich gefragt, ob ich ihm mein neues Fahrrad leihen kann.
4. I würde gerne wissen, wie man diesen Schrank aufstellen soll.
5. Wir werden sehr bald wissen, ob er die Prüfung bestanden hat.
6. Bitte zeige mir, wo ich meine Koffer hintun kann/soll.
7. Weißt du, seit wann Ann zurück ist?
8. Wir haben keine Ahnung, wo wir dieses Jahr unsere Ferien verbringen sollen.

Übung 84:
1. to give him the book.
2. to clean the glasses carefully.
3. not to use his bike.
4. to open the window.
5. not to come home late.
6. to give her some advice.
7. not to forget to show their parents the letter.
8. to tell them a story.

9. to bring some milk if she goes to the supermarket.
10. not to put on her new shoes.

Übung 85:

1. Der Lehrer sagt Mary, dass sie ihm das Buch geben soll.
2. Frau Elliot sagt ihrem Sohn, dass er die Gläser sorgfältig putzen soll.
3. Peter sagt seinem kleinen Bruder, dass er sein Fahrrad nicht nehmen soll / verbietet seinem kleinen Bruder sein Fahrrad zu nehmen.
4. Herr Mason bittet einen Schüler das Fenster zu öffnen.
5. Herr Brown sagt seiner Tochter, dass sie nicht zu spät kommen soll / befiehlt seiner Tochter nicht zu spät zu kommen.
6. Mary bittet Susan, ihr einen Rat zu geben.
7. Mr Mason sagt seiner Klasse, dass sie nicht vergessen soll, ihren Eltern den Brief zu zeigen / ermahnt seine Klasse nicht zu vergessen, ihren Eltern den Brief zu zeigen.
8. Nellie bittet ihren Großvater, ihnen eine Geschichte zu erzählen.
9. Marys Mutter sagt ihr, dass sie Milch mitbringen soll, wenn sie zum Supermarkt geht.
10. Und sie sagt ihr, dass sie nicht ihre neuen Schuhe anziehen soll.

Übung 86:

1. Peter's mother tells him to turn up the radio.
2. Mrs Simson asks Mike to carry her bag.
3. Tom's father has told him not to go to school by bike.
4. I've told you again and again to take the keys with you.
5. Why don't you ask him to ring you up?
6. Please tell him to buy some flowers.
7. Bob orders his dog to bring back the ball.
8. The doctor advises Mary to stay in bed for one week.
9. He tells her not to run around.
10. We must ask Kate to lend us her tent.

Übung 87:

1. had bought 2. would fly 3. can't help 4. wasn't 5. doesn't want 6. hadn't ordered 7. might be

Übung 88:

1. if she could help him to prepare the party
2. that Peter will help you
3. that he had been playing for the same football team
4. if/whether Ann had already found
5. that she lived
6. that they were planning
7. that they had been able to hide ... it had started
8. that he doesn't know
9. that they had been watching TV when they had heard
10. that Joe was going to New York

Übung 89:

1. that he might let him play
2. not to walk alone
3. where I had learned
4. when to collect Joe
5. that he was so glad to see her
6. to look after her/his flowers ... she/he was
7. how to answer these questions
8. that Mike and Mary had just left ... they would be back
9. not to be late ... the train would leave
10. that she hadn't been able to do

Übung 90:

1. In the middle ages people simply didn't want to believe that the earth isn't flat.
2. Mr Jackson was surprised (to see) that his daughter Evelyne plays the piano so well.
3. Pat told us that in Germany school already starts at 8 o'clock.
4. She also told us that a lot of German people didn't know that England and Great Britain isn't the same.
5. She said that the cities she had visited last year are very famous.
6. Pat told us that most people there speak English well.
7. She said that many rare flowers grow on the mountains.

Übung 91:

1. he was going to visit his son George ... the next/following day.
2. had had an accident the week before.
3. had run into him ... there in front of their house.
4. would come home that afternoon ... he had been in hospital for three weeks.
5. they had had dinner ... that restaurant was ... they might go there again the next/following Friday.
6. couldn't help me that day ... I hadn't asked him some days before.

Übung 92:

1. Ben said he might come to us the next/following day.
2. Ben's mother told him to do his homework first.
3. We asked him why he hadn't come by bus.
4. Jack had told us that he wanted to go to university the next/following month.
5. Peter always says that he likes playing hockey.
6. Nobody told him that his dog had been injured some hours before.
7. We didn't know where to buy the tickets.
8. Mary didn't tell us that she would take part in the tournament, too.
9. Her trainer had told her not to say anything.

Übung 93:

1. when 2. if 3. If 4. when 5. when 6. if

Übung 94:

1. go 2. will give, find 3. aren't 4. won't, show, don't ask 5. will you say, asks 6. agree 7. has found 8. won't find, has moved 9. finds, will buy

Übung 95:

1. the restaurant isn't too expensive.
2. will pass the exam.
3. he asks you.
4. will/can see the castle.
5. you like him?
6. must take a taxi.
7. you must give him a chance / give him a chance.
8. will help you.
9. you go by car?
10. I will give a party.

Übung 96:

1. If Pat really comes to see us we must show her the sights of our town.
2. If you haven't done your homework again, Mr Mason will inform your parents.
3. We will see more of the countryside, if we go by bike.
4. You can only help him if you talk with him.
5. You can save a lot of time if you do your homework carefully.
6. If you work faster, you can play with your friends earlier.
7. If we don't find a solution, we'll have to dismiss a lot of workers.
8. If Mary has to stay in hospital any longer, she will get even more problems at school.
9. It will be easier for her if we help her then.
10. Will you go to Birmingham, if Peter invites you, Susan?

Übung 97:

1. tried 2. wouldn't find, didn't have 3. didn't do, couldn't afford 4. couldn't, would enjoy 5. would do, weren't 6. had 7. were, would talk 8. would you like, had 9. would be, didn't have

Übung 98:

1. I had the time.
2. will go for a walk.
3. you switched on the light.
4. could make a cake.
5. he asked you?
6. I were you.
7. I were my own boss.
8. will be better.
9. he asked me.
10. read the text again.

Übung 99:

1. If I did, I would have to invite Susan, too.
2. If he didn't, he would lose one year.
3. If I didn't, Mike wouldn't get it tomorrow.
4. If I did, I couldn't sleep tonight.
5. If I did, he would surely have an accident.

Übung 100:

1. If we lived in the country, we would grow our own vegetable.
2. If he weren't away on business, he could go to the cinema with us.
3. The children could go skating if the lake were frozen.
4. Would your brother be angry if you took his bike without asking him?
5. If they were my children, they wouldn't be allowed to see this film.
6. If there weren't so little traffic, we wouldn't get to the airport in time.
7. If she sold her surfboard now, she wouldn't get much money for it.
8. If we went to the cinema tomorrow, we could play tennis today.
9. If you agreed, I would buy the tickets.
10. We would recognize him at once if he were standing in front of us now.

Übung 101:

1. had caught, wouldn't have missed
2. had been, wouldn't have broken
3. had studied, would have got
4. would have left earlier, hadn't rained
5. hadn't gone, might have lost
6. Would you have taken, had offered
7. would have heard, hadn't been taking
8. would have been, hadn't been organized
9. hadn't been operated on, might have died.
10. hadn't been, wouldn't have got

Übung 102:

1. If he hadn't drunk so much, he wouldn't have run into the tree.
2. If they hadn't been running, they wouldn't have been so thirsty.
3. If my parents hadn't paid a part of it, I wouldn't have been able to buy this bike.
4. If the coat hadn't been so expensive, she would have bought it.
5. If he hadn't been so weak, we would have told him the truth.
6. If Mr Johnson hadn't arrived so late his wife would have woken him up.

Übung 103:

1. She would have come with us if she hadn't been ill.
2. Pat wouldn't have been able to go to Germany if she hadn't learned German so well.
3. If Mike hadn't reminded Peter, he would have forgotten Susan's birthday.
4. The thieves would have robbed the whole house if the police hadn't come in time.
5. But we wouldn't have been able to call the police if the dog hadn't barked.
6. What would you have done if the police hadn't come?

7. If the alarm clock hadn't rung, we would have overslept.
8. If we hadn't slept so long we would have seen the sunrise.
9. Joe wouldn't have gone to America if he had found a job here.
10. We wouldn't have found this hotel if Peter hadn't recommended it to us.

Übung 104:

1. wouldn't have to hurry 2. could pass 3. had invited 4. had taken 5. wouldn't let

Übung 105:

1. We could help you, if you had informed us in time.
2. Mrs Johnson will be very sad, if she has to leave her flat.
3. She would be relieved if she knew where to find a new flat.
4. She would already have finished the house long ago, if she had had enough money.
5. What would you do, if you had won the competition?
6. If Jenny isn't at home, she will be at her friend's.
7. If he had been more successful, she would have married him.
8. But I wonder if they were happy if they had married.
9. I wouldn't buy this pullover even if I had enough money.
10. We might play table tennis if he came here.

Teil B

Test 1:

a) 1. are running 2. have known 3. was reading, rang 4. is raining 5. had 6. has been talking 7. we'll be laughing, have

b) 1. Did you play, were 2. have been looking, saw, was lying 3. have just reached or: are just reaching 4. are just having 5. will fly 6. will be sitting

c)
1. I couldn't go to the cinema last week. I was preparing my exam.
2. At the moment they are playing this song again and again.
3. Fred lives in London now. But at the moment he is visiting his parents / is staying at his parents' here.
4. Yesterday he promised to call me. But I have been waiting for his call since this morning.
5. We were waiting for the bus when he spoke to us.

Test 2:

a) 1.C 2.B 3.C 4.A 5.C 6.B 7.A

b)
1. Do you know when the train leaves tomorrow?
2. Will you see her tomorrow? – No, I'm going to repair / I'll be repairing my bike tomorrow.
3. Have you got the tickets? – Oh, no. I'll fetch them at once.
4. What are you doing this evening/tonight? – I'm going to the cinema with friends.
5. I think you'll like the film. I'm going to see it next weekend, too.
6. I'm going to Paris next Saturday.

Test 3:

a) 1. know 2. is, has been lying 3. is, haven't seen 4. know, has told 5. have you been working 6. doesn't talk, have always understood

b) 1. has won, has been practising 2. shows, has ever succeeded 3. have been looking, have been / are reading 4. has lost, is trying 5. has broken down, don't you buy

c)
1. I haven't been smoking for two months now.
2. Since when have you had your driver's licence?
3. We always go by bus. But today we have missed it.
4. They have always been living next to each other. But now they are quarreling.

Test 4:

a)
1. I haven't smoked since the doctor told me to stop it.

2. Yesterday he promised to come but he hasn't appeared yet.
3. We ordered a bottle of champagne after he had passed his exam.
4. Mary didn't know if Mike had been injured in the accident, too.
5. Since I bought this book I have read it three times.
6. They had promised to deliver the cupboard in time but we only got it yesterday.
7. I asked Peter to help me to repair my bike because he had already repaired his own one.

b) 1. was, hadn't seen 2. opened, sat down 3. bought 4. haven't you brought 5. was, returned, had already gone 6. have missed, broke down

c)
1. Tom had already left when I arrived at his place. He had taken a taxi.
2. Since when have you known that they married in Paris?
3. She behaved as if she had never seen him before.
4. We have already been wondering for a long time if they took the right decision then.

Test 5:
a)
1.C 2.B 3.A 4.C 5.A 6.B 7.C 8.B

b)
1. We had to answer very difficult questions.
2. Only a few are said to have passed the test.
3. Peter didn't have to stay until the end, he was allowed to leave earlier.
4. You were to bring the books already yesterday.
5. You needn't worry about this.

Test 6:
a) 1. has been looked for 2. will be opened 3. are just being opened 4. was published 5. must be repaired 6. should be opened 7. by Chris 8. was being observed 9. couldn't be found

b)
1. The new cinema will be opened tomorrow evening.
2. nobody had been injured in the accident.
3. had to be taken to hospital by the ambulance men.
4. The missing child hasn't been found yet by the police.
5. The witnesses have been questioned for two hours now.
6. It must have been stolen.
7. Service is included in the bill.
8. The exhibition was still being prepared ...
9. the decision won't be taken before next week.
10. in the end he was elected president.

c)

1. This tree will have to be cut down.
2. The street was built one year ago.
3. Since when has she been called Billy?
4. The children were thanked for their attention by the Lady mayor herself.
5. We will be asked a lot of questions.
6. She was shown different dresses by the shop assistant. Different dresses were shown to her by ...

Test 7:

a) 1. that his father <u>was</u> in hospital 2. that he <u>would</u> come home 3. if he <u>had already seen</u> 4. what we <u>had been doing</u> when the accident <u>had happened</u> 5. that I <u>hadn't been practising</u> enough 6. that he <u>was</u> in town again. 7. where they <u>had hidden</u> the money? 8. where they <u>could</u> find the basketball?

b)

1. that he didn't think that this colour suited her.
2. that he would help them the next/following day.
3. not to wait with my visit until the next/following week.
4. that he didn't like / doesn't like that sort of cake.
5. that she hoped she could go to Germany (the) next year.

c)

1. where to find the petrol station.
2. how to do that exercise.
3. where the trousers were that he had bought the day before.
4. by when to finish the German paper / they were to have finished the German paper.
6. who had told me that lie.

Test 8:

a)

1. If you asked him
2. if I didn't have to work today.
3. We would have got
4. if she hadn't stumbled.
5. Mary can get
6. even if it keeps ringing.
7. Would you join
8. He wouldn't be so happy
9. If she had had the possibility when she was young
10. if I could.

b) 1. were 2. needed 3. will improve 4. wasn't raining 5. would have organized 6. come 7. wouldn't be 8. wasn't raining 9. had known 10. would understand